"Deciding if homeschooling is right for your family just got easier with this warm, entertaining, information-packed portrayal of its flexibility, diversity, triumphs, and challenges. Grab a cup of tea and enjoy!"

LINDA DOBSON, AUTHOR OF *THE FIRST YEAR OF HOMESCHOOLING YOUR CHILD: YOUR COMPLETE GUIDE TO GETTING OFF TO THE RIGHT START*

"Regardless of your religious beliefs or your personal approach to homeschooling, this is a very important book—both for veteran homeschooling families and those who are just *thinking* about homeschooling. As I read, I felt even more connected to the wonderful community of homeschoolers and I also found new ways to help my children learn."

ELIZABETH KANNA, COAUTHOR OF *HOMESCHOOLING FOR SUCCESS: HOW PARENTS CAN CREATE A SUPERIOR EDUCATION FOR THEIR CHILD*

LISA
WHELCHEL

SO YOU'RE
THINKING ABOUT
Homeschooling

Fifteen Families Show How You Can Do It!

Multnomah® Publishers *Sisters, Oregon*

SO YOU'RE THINKING ABOUT HOMESCHOOLING
published by Multnomah Publishers, Inc.

© 2005 by Lisa Whelchel
International Standard Book Number: 1-59052-511-6
Previously 1-59052-085-8

Cover image of Lisa Whelchel by Claudia Kunin
Cover image of children by Corbis

Unless otherwise indicated, Scripture quotations are from *The Amplified Bible* © 1965,
1987 by Zondervan Publishing House. *The Amplified New Testament* © 1958, 1987 by the
Lockman Foundation.

Focus on the Family ® is a registered trademark of Focus on the Family.

Multnomah is a trademark of Multnomah Publishers, Inc.,
and is registered in the U.S. Patent and Trademark Office.
The colophon is a trademark of Multnomah Publishers, Inc.

Printed in the United States of America

For information:
MULTNOMAH PUBLISHERS, INC. · P.O. BOX 1720 · SISTERS, OR 97759

Library of Congress Cataloging-in-Publication Data

Whelchel, Lisa.
    So you're thinking about homeschooling / by Lisa Whelchel.
        p. cm.
    ISBN 1-59052-085-8
    ISBN 1-59052-511-6
    1. Home schooling—United States. 2. Education—Parent participation—
United States.
    I. Title.
    LC40.W517 2003
    371.04'2—dc21

                                    2002156086

05 06 07 08 09—10 9 8 7 6 5 4 3 2 1

It is a privilege to dedicate this book to
my husband and partner,
Steve.
Thank you for taking such good care of us
and providing a home where we can live, love, and learn.
We are honored to call you the head of our household.

PROVERBS 17:6
"…the glory of children is their fathers."

Table of Contents

Foreword

A faithful friend is an invaluable part of every home-schooler's life. A friend buoys your spirits when you are facing tasks that seem too big for the moment. She tells you the truth when you need to hear it. And most of all, she listens and understands.

Lisa Whelchel proves herself a faithful friend to those who are contemplating the big question: Should we homeschool our kids?

Lisa tells you the truth about homeschooling. She has listened to the joys and tribulations of more than a thousand homeschooling families, and by taking you into the lives of several composite families, she paints an accurate picture of the struggles you can expect and the sacrifices which may be required. But most importantly, Lisa is telling you the truth when she says that whatever the struggle, the rewards make it all worthwhile.

I have met Lisa, Steve, and their homeschooled children, and I can tell you she is truthful about them as well—her kids are just as delightful as she says. But Lisa is careful to make a couple of other very important points that you should keep in mind as you consider the needs of your own family:

1. Every child is truly different.
2. There is no one right way to homeschool.

If you decide to homeschool, pick an approach that is right for your family's situation and for the needs of your children.

First of all, let me assure you that every family portrayed in this book is quite lawful in their approach to homeschooling. No state mandates a particular form of teaching (e.g., traditional, textbook, classical). While there are legal details that must be considered—for example, some states do require that the child's own parent do the teaching—any parents who choose to diligently homeschool their children have a constitutional right to do so.

So how do you pick the right approach for teaching *your* children? You can visit a number of websites or go to a curriculum fair and learn about the various options. But one of the best ways is to hear from the people who have walked this path before, people who have already explored and family-tested the many different possibilities. The stories in this book are told from the hearts of the moms and dads who have lived them.

So You're Thinking About Homeschooling is a great introduction to home education. Open the book and you will also find a good friend in Lisa.

Michael Farris
President, Patrick Henry College
Founder and Chairman,
Home School Legal Defense Association

Acknowledgments

They say you should save the best for last. If that is true, then this should be the final page. Acknowledging the gratitude I feel for all those who help me is my favorite part of writing books.

Steve. You put the home in homeschooling for me. I'm grateful that I get to partner with you in ministry, family, and life.

Tucker, Haven, and Clancy. I'm so proud of you! I am extremely blessed to have the luxury of staying home with you all day. What a joy to be your mom!

Anastasia Jové. You are the young adult every homeschool mom hopes her child grows up to become. Your care and example have been a gift to my children and me.

Megan Morrow, Jan Dickson, and Laura Pierce. Thank you for homeschooling my kids while I wrote a book about homeschooling my kids.

Cyber Prayer Warriors. Thank you for lifting this book and me before the Father with such faithfulness. I have rested in your prayers and His answers.

Robert Miller and Summerfield Suites by Wyndham. My home away from home these last few months. Thank you for providing such a comfortable place to write.

Multnomah Publishers. I am very impressed by you, each and every one. Don, your sensitivity to follow the Lord's leading at all costs has allowed Him to build a company of integrity and excellence.

Bill Jensen. I can't imagine myself writing books without you—I don't even want to think about it. You have stood by me from the very beginning, and I sure hope you'll stay with me till the end.

David and Peggy Webb and Renee DeLoriea. With the mind of an editor and the soul of a parent, you each have imprinted the words in this book with both your skill and heart.

Focus on the Family. For years I have supported you and what you are doing. I'm humbled that you would believe so much in me.

Ron Smith. I've always looked up to you in business. Looking down at you lately, because you've been on your knees, has only built you up more in my eyes.

Michael Farris, Mary Pride, Elizabeth Kanna, Linda Dobson, Richard and Cindee Grant. Some of you are good friends; others are acquaintances; and still others I have never even met. And yet, you have all influenced my family more than you could know. You are my homeschool heroes.

The "families" in this book. I wish I had room to personally mention all one thousand names of those who shared their stories with me through e-mail. You know who you are. Please accept my thanks, especially the one hundred moms and dads who talked with me on the phone.

Carla Calvert, Anita Koller, Susan LaBounty, and Stephanie Micke. There were some areas of homeschooling where I would have been lost if it weren't for the expertise of these extremely helpful friends. Thank you for coming to my rescue.

Finally, I would like to thank the entire homeschooling community. It has been my pleasure to proudly declare myself a homeschooler. It is a privilege to hold the torch high that others might see the difference you and your children are making for the future of our world.

Chapter One

Let's Talk

S o, you're thinking about homeschooling. Congratulations! Even considering taking a road less traveled requires courage. May I walk the first few steps of this journey with you? It often helps to have someone beside you who has "been there, done that." Let me assure you up front that the homeschooling path is not as daunting as it probably seems to you at this moment. Fear of the unknown is always the scariest part.

I promise I will stay with you long enough for you to feel confident in whatever decision you ultimately make. Yes, you heard me correctly—*I'm not assuming that you will end up choosing to homeschool.* Homeschooling is not necessarily the best option for everyone. But I do believe it is such a fabulous alternative that no one should reject it without first looking full into the face of it.

Many people have a preconceived idea of what home-schooling is all about. They think that because they don't fit a particular profile, they are excluded from seriously considering the option. But the truth is that there really is no such thing as a typical homeschooling family. Think about it: Any family who is willing to go against the flow of the traditional public school setting is already thinking outside the box. You're probably just a bit off-center yourself. I like that in a person.

So what does the average homeschooling family look like? That's kind of like asking, "What does the average person look like?" Well, we have two eyes, a nose, and a mouth; apart from that, we all have a distinctive look. The same thing is true for the face of homeschooling. You will find a few similar features: for example, parents who want a good education for their children and feel there is no one with a more vested interest in teaching their child than themselves. Beyond that, each family is unique.

What's so funny about the notion of a "typical" homeschooling family is that most of us don't even look the same from year to year. We may begin by homeschooling an only child and graduate with a full house. At any given time, our primary goals may be preparation for higher education, building character, developing closer family relationships, or an emphasis on real-life learning. Most of the time we are enthusiastic about homeschooling; at other times we feel like failures at it.

Not only is the face of a homeschooling family often changing, but the makeup is even harder to describe. Probably the most common combination is a working father and stay-at-home mother with multiple children. But you might be surprised at the number of single mothers, full-time dads, teaching grandmas, traveling families, and former public schoolteachers who have chosen to homeschool, many with just one child.

And forget trying to figure out *how* the typical family approaches home education. There are as many different philosophies, curriculum options, and teaching styles as there are reasons for homeschooling. Did you know that many homeschoolers never open a textbook? For many, their most important tool is a library card. A family may be passionate about the principle approach, the Charlotte Mason method, on-line academies, or unschooling. Or maybe like me, they try a little bit of everything until they find the perfect style of learning for each child, only to have *life* happen and force them to try something completely new the next year. Try watching *our* family to figure out what the face of a homeschooling family looks like, and you'll quickly become dizzy.

The bottom line is, you have to find what works for *your* family. In order to do that, you need to know what's out there. I could give you a list of curriculum companies, teaching methods, and homeschool statistics. But there are already dozens of books on homeschooling, full of impressive facts and information. These are written to address the mind.

I'm guessing that it is for the love of a child that you are even reading this book in the first place. That is why I have chosen to speak to your heart, using stories.

Beginning with my own, I want to introduce you to fifteen families in unique situations who have all chosen to homeschool for different reasons, using a variety of learning methods. You will notice that although our family purposefully homeschools from a Christian worldview, the homes in most of the other stories could be of any faith or no particular faith at all. Same goes for the curriculum choices portrayed here. Some curricula are obviously written from a Judeo-Christian perspective; others focus primarily on higher education or great literature.

You may be surprised to learn that public-school bashing is not high on my list of priorities. Granted, many of the families in this book reflect disappointment in one or more aspects of public education, but the majority of reasons represented have more to do with unique home-life situations. I have no personal experience with the public school system, and my only experience with a private Christian school was fabulous. So no, I'm not anti—traditional school. I'm pro-home-school.

That is why I can't wait to introduce you to some of my homeschooling "friends." I use quotation marks because although I consider to be friends the more than one thousand parents I interviewed via e-mail and the nearly one hundred I talked with on the phone, you would not actually recognize any of them in the following stories. Each family portrayed here is a composite, made up from bits and pieces of the stories of actual people, in verifiable situations, teaching tried-and-true homeschooling methods.

Remember, this book is not a "How to Get Started" manual, a compendium of laws and statistics, or an exhaustive curriculum resource guide. It is a "Let's rap lightly on the door of homeschooling and peek inside before we decide whether we are ready to move in" kind of book. My hope is that by the end of the book and the parade of homes, you may identify a family situation and teaching approach from these stories that resonates with your personality and philosophy of education.

But first, I want to invite you over to my house.

Chapter Two

Welcome to My House

Welcome to my house! Come on in. May I grab you a Diet Coke? Can I tempt you with a frozen waffle fresh from the toaster? No? Well then, just have a seat for a minute while I finish loading the breakfast dishes in the dishwasher. Oops, I'm sorry—are you stuck there? Here, let me wipe that syrup off the table. I have a better idea. Let me get my kids to finish cleaning up the kitchen and we can talk in the living room.

So you're thinking about homeschooling? Well, you've come to the right place. I love homeschooling! I'll be happy to offer any advice I can from my own personal experience, and later, if you still have questions, then I have plenty of friends who have answers. (And they will probably offer you more than a soggy waffle to go along with their perspective.)

But enough about them, let's talk about you by talking about us. I remember being exactly where you are right now when I was first thinking about homeschooling. I understand what must be swirling around in your mind if you are even considering educating your children at home: Is it even legal? How much will it cost? Can I really teach my children? Will I ruin them for life? What about what I *don't* know? What about what I don't know that I don't know? Will my kids become social misfits? What will my mother-in-law think? Will I go crazy in the process? What if I need to work outside the home? Must I have twelve children, raise goats, and bake my own bread? Where do I start?

You've already started. Think about it. Who taught your child how to walk? how to use a spoon? how to go potty like a big boy? Did you send your children away to an institution to learn their ABC's, count their ten little Indians, or speak in complete sentences? I've considered hiring a professional to teach my children to brush their teeth, clean their rooms, and get along with each other, but I doubt it would yield any better results. What makes parents think that once our children reach the age of five, we are no longer capable of teaching them?

Thankfully, I didn't have a chance to ask myself this question before I found myself homeschooling without even realizing it. Wait a minute—let me back up a few years and start from the beginning.

I filmed the last episode of *The Facts of Life* in March 1988. I married Steve in July 1988, got pregnant in May 1989, and proceeded to have children in 1990, 1991, and 1992.

It was at this point that I left show business to become a stay-at-home wife and mother. Not that this decision was particularly noble; the truth is I couldn't get a job. As an actress it is kind of hard to go on auditions if you are either pregnant, nursing, in the OB/GYN office, or in my case, all three at the same time. I eventually realized that God was no longer blessing my acting career because He wanted me to be the one to raise the children He had so graciously, and quickly, given us. I was to find His blessing at home.

So being the type A person I am, I jumped in with both feet. The toddler years were heavily scheduled with Mommy & Me classes, Sunday school, and Gymboree groups. Television viewing was limited to *Sesame Street,* Barney, and educational videos. Afternoons were spent finger painting, playing toy instruments, and building things from blocks and LEGOs.

I started preparing Tucker for higher education—kindergarten—about the time he graduated from diapers to Batman underwear. He was eager to move on to something a bit more challenging than writing his name and singing his ABC's. I called my Aunt Polly, who was a schoolteacher in Texas, for advice. She recommended I find a good phonics program and some colorful math workbooks. So Tucker and I "played school" for an hour every day while his little sisters were down for a nap. When it was finally time to enroll him in kindergarten, he could read the longest of short-vowel words.

Here was my dilemma: Was Tucker ready for formal schooling or was he *too* ready? At this point he had not been diagnosed with ADHD (attention deficit hyperactivity disorder), but all the signs were there. Would it be possible for him to sit still in a class, especially if he already knew everything they were teaching?

Since kindergarten enrollment isn't mandatory in the

state of California, and because we couldn't afford to enroll him in private school, Steve and I decided to keep him home another year and see if he would outgrow his "rowdy boy" phase. In the meantime Haven, who was almost four years old, joined us in the schoolroom (a.k.a. the kitchen table), while Clancy, two and a half, worked at her desk/high chair.

Three years into this experiment, we were having so much fun, you couldn't have paid me to send my kids to school. Before you could say "no college degree," I had succeeded in teaching a kindergartener, first-grader, and second-grader how to "read, 'rite, and 'rithmetic."

During this time it became clear that homeschooling was the right choice for my children, although for different reasons. I was able to tailor Tucker's education to fit the special needs of an ADHD child. True, there were many days when I had to call on the infinite love of a mother for the patience to teach him, but I can only imagine the kind of trouble he might have had at school.

Haven would have no doubt soared in a traditional school setting—except for the fact that her wings would have to be clipped in order to hold her back with the rest of the flock. At home the sky was the limit, and she flew through her studies.

We were having so much fun, you couldn't have paid me to send my kids to school.

Clancy was still a momma's girl. I learned that her tender soul needed protecting, and I was grateful for the luxury of a few more years at home to prepare her for the harsh realities of life.

With the three R's firmly in place, it was time to shake

things up a bit. We added more layers with less structure. Sounds like a blueprint for destruction, but it actually turned out to be highly productive. We gathered every morning for an hour around the kitchen table, and I read "hero" stories while the children practiced their handwriting. We worked on Bible memory verses, sang praise songs, and took turns praying.

From there, each child found a "studying spot." This might be under the dining room table, behind the couch, or outside on the trampoline. Many a morning would find me hunkering down under a blanket draped over a couple of chairs teaching fractions and pronouns. After our daily dose of math and language arts, it was time to move on to the fun stuff.

The remainder of the morning was given to open-ended exploration of a specific subject. Monday was American history. Tuesday was science. Wednesday was creative writing. Thursday was devoted to educational games, and Friday was reserved for field trips. We discovered that it was a lot more fun to dig into one subject for a full day than to scratch the surface of each subject on five separate days.

Halfway into that school year, life got even *funner*. (Does it worry you at all that I'm the one teaching grammar to my children?) A good friend of mine became ill and was not able to continue homeschooling her children. I offered to teach them while she recovered, and I suddenly had a bona fide classroom of five students! I was tempted to purchase a blackboard, American flag, and a bell to ring. But I stopped short of putting on a hair net and serving sloppy joes and chocolate milk for lunch.

There was nothing orthodox about that school year (except maybe for the fact that we studied and observed each of the Jewish holidays for Bible class). When the van Gogh exhibit came to town, we read about Vincent's life and then spent a day at the art museum. We took field trips to the transportation museum and the children's science center, and I enrolled the kids in music appreciation classes at the Hollywood Bowl. Graduation was celebrated there with a family picnic under the stars while the Los Angeles Philharmonic performed Gustav Holst's *The Planets*. Looking back, this was our favorite year of school.

Shortly after beginning the next school year, just about the time we were feeling like we had a handle on life, I was asked to write my first book, *Creative Correction*. Suddenly, our best laid plans flew out the window. I tried teaching in the morning and writing in the afternoon, but my manuscript deadline was looming larger and ever nearer. I tried bringing in a tutor to teach the kids while I wrote upstairs. But as any mom can attest, it's next to impossible to carry on a complete conversation on the phone with kids in the house, much less try to carry on a conversation on paper.

I finally gave in and let Steve drop the kids off at their grandmother's house every day on his way to work. I would prepare each of them a folder of workbook sheets, and Grandmother, who had spent the last four years home-schooling my younger brother, would supervise their studies. Thankfully, she's a game-playing, bike-riding, book-loving, cookie-baking type of grandma, so they learned many things with her that I couldn't have taught them myself. They stayed on track with their times tables and spelling rules, but the most valuable lesson they learned was that they can always find unconditional love and acceptance at Grandmother's house.

And I learned that I wasn't able to adequately teach my young children and write a book at the same time. So before I started writing *The Facts of Life (and Other Lessons My Father Taught Me)*, we made the agonizing decision to place the kids in a more traditional school setting. We found a wonderful Christian school that many of their friends attended, and we enjoyed our first official back-to-school shopping spree. I must admit it was awfully fun to pick out backpacks, lunch boxes and number two pencils. Car pools, homework, and sack lunches got a bit old around mid-November, but all in all, it was a fabulous experience.

I was so proud of my children! Despite their inexperience with institutional learning, they excelled not only in the classroom but also on the playground (and we all know that sometimes the schoolyard is the more difficult arena). Even so, there were many nights when I sat on the edge of a child's bed while he or she cried in my arms, "I want my old life and my old mommy back!" We all missed homeschooling.

Ironically, the next year we didn't homeschool either— we motor-homeschooled! The whole family hopped into an Allegro Bus RV and set out to discover America and, more importantly, discover each other. For one full year, we took the ultimate field trip, visiting living history museums, state capitals, factory tours, friends, family, and churches all across America. In my opinion, this was homeschooling at its finest.

And that brings us to our first year of junior high. This year school again looks quite different from the previous ones. Tucker, Haven, and Clancy are enrolled in the Alpha Omega On-line Academy. They do all of their work on the computer and then send it, via the Internet, to their teacher in cyberspace. She grades it and sends it back by the next morning, with corrections, notes, and assignments for the day.

As much as I prefer being a hands-on home-schooler, I've had to accept the fact that I only have two hands with which to take care of my family, homeschool, write books, oversee MomTime Ministries, and update LisaWhelchel.com. The on-line academy is exactly what the Great Physician ordered for this season of my life and ministry. The curriculum is challenging enough to hone the kids' independent study skills while freeing me up to work at home as I superintend their schoolwork.

Wow! What in the world will *next* year look like?

Are you more confused than ever? Perhaps you're wondering how the children have adapted to our near-annual variations on homeschooling. How effective is the education they've received? Well, since you asked, allow me to brag on my little darlings a bit. On standardized tests, they have all tested in the ninetieth percentile and, in many subjects, the ninety-ninth. But homeschooling has brought out their best in many areas, not just academics.

Tucker does very well in school and is working a year ahead in language arts. He has an outstanding vocabulary, but where he really excels is socially. He can converse with anyone about anything, regardless of age differences.

Everyone wants to be his friend because he's so much fun to talk to and be around. On the flip side, because he is so verbal, we are forever working with him on learning to think before he speaks.

Haven is a natural-born leader and is currently doing two years of school at once with the goal of finishing high school by age fourteen. She has already visited Patrick Henry College in Virginia, where she plans to attend and pursue a career in politics, with an eye toward becoming the first female president of the United States. She thrives on setting high goals and challenging herself to meet them. Since she was in the second grade, her idea of fun in the car has been for me to make up algebra problems for her to solve. School comes so easily to her that she sometimes works too fast and is prone to making careless mistakes, so we are taking the time to teach her to take her time.

Clancy is wise beyond her years. She is a diligent student, but she also has uncanny spiritual insights for such a young girl. She loves the Lord and asks many deep questions about His Word. She is also a wonderful little prayer warrior. Clancy excels academically because she tries hard and double-checks her work, and yet she lacks self-confidence. Because her sister is gifted intellectually, and because her brother's personality is larger-than-life, Clancy tends to underestimate her own gifts and abilities, even though she often makes the best grades in the family.

I can not boast in my children's accomplishments as a testament to any remarkable teaching skill on my part. The truth is, I only went as far as the sixth grade in a traditional school setting. I moved to California when I was twelve years old and, as a child actress, bounced between on-set tutoring and unschooling before settling into an accelerated course of home study and earning my high school diploma.

That makes what happened yesterday at the post office all the more amazing. The kids were waiting in the lobby for me while I stood in line to mail some packages. Unbeknownst to me, a police officer approached my children and asked them why they were not in school in the middle of the day. They explained that they were home-schooled. So the policeman grilled them with about a dozen questions like, "Who was the sixteenth president?" "What happened on December 7, 1941?" and "Which state has the right to become its own country at any time?" They must have passed the test because as we were walking out of the post office, the policeman was driving off. When he saw us, he backed up, rolled down his window, and shouted, "Good job, Mom! Your kids are extremely intelligent."

This may sound like I'm bragging on my children, but I am really touting the wonders of homeschooling.

Hopefully, from my story you can see that no matter how unusual your circumstances may be, how unqualified you feel to teach, or how unique your children are, you can still homeschool—and successfully! The more I think about it, the more I believe that introducing you to some other homeschooling families will help you get a clearer picture of what the homeschool adventure is all about. Do you have time to meet a few of my friends?

Great! Just let me call Anastasia, our babysitter up the street, and we'll be on our way. I just know you'll love my friend Holly. She's kind of new to homeschooling, and like you, there was a time when she wasn't at all sure about it. But I'll let *her* tell you her story. She's offered to meet us over coffee.

Let's go!

Chapter Three

There's No Place Like Homeschool

Hi, I'm Holly. Thanks for meeting me at Starbucks. What a treat! No, put your money away. This one's on me. What'll you have? Are you sure? All right then, she'll just have a tall drip. I'll have a half-caff/quad/grandé in a venti cup, organic, one-eighty, easy foam, with whip, four-pump mocha.

Let's sit down over here where it's quieter.

The kids are with their dad at the animal shelter, picking out a family dog. I'm not thrilled about the idea, but in the meantime I get two blessed hours of freedom, so I'm not complaining. Does it sound like I'm complaining? I don't mean to. I love being with my kids, but that doesn't mean that I can't enjoy a moment alone or have coffee with another mom.

Believe me, I've been on the other side of the "working outside the home" fence, and the grass is definitely *not* greener. I found it to be so dry that I became as brittle as the under-cared-for lawn. Before I laid aside my career to become a stay-at-home wife and homeschooling mom, life was so hectic that there just wasn't time to make sure everyone was getting enough "water" and attention. Oh, I did my best and we all survived, but who wants to simply exist when you can enjoy life with your family—on your own beautiful green lawn.

THE STRESS–FULL SCHEDULE

We used to be up every morning by six o'clock. My husband, Ted, was up and out the door by six-thirty. Hunter, Sascha, and Madison would get up, get dressed, grab a quick bowl of cereal, look for the lost baseball glove, recover from the bad-hair-day meltdown, bicker and fight, and ask the standard "Where did you put my backpack?" question. I gave the customary "Wherever you laid it down last" response. All this happened while I attempted to shower, blow-dry my hair, hop around the room putting on panty hose, and get dressed so that we could all get out the door by seven.

The kids spent the next hour on the school bus, and I spent that time in traffic, nursing my coffee, putting on my makeup, and taking care of business on my cell phone—not necessarily all at the same time. (But not necessarily *not,* either.) While the kids were at school, I was at work worrying about Sascha falling behind in math, anxious about the new attitudes surfacing in Hunter, and feeling guilty thinking, *What if Madison really was sick and not just trying to get out of going to school this morning?*

After school the kids took the bus home—another hour wasted—and stayed by themselves from four o'clock to five-thirty, when Ted got home. The idea was for them to get their homework done during that time, but that was seldom a reality. In the meantime, I would pick up something for dinner on the way home, and we would eat it in the car on the way to gymnastics, soccer practice, or math tutoring. Even though we tried to limit their activities to one per child, it seemed we still had someplace to be almost every evening.

And then there was still homework, at least an hour of it, maybe more. We rarely got into bed before ten. By then we were all exhausted, and I had very little left over to give to Ted. Not that he was awake when I got to bed, anyway. As you can probably imagine, our relationship vacillated between strained and growing apart. What was happening to our family? What could I do to change its course? How could I find more hours in a day?

I'll Never Homeschool

The thought of homeschooling crossed my mind briefly, but just as quickly I brushed it away. Ted's cousin Eliza homeschooled her kids, and they were geeky little robots— I certainly didn't want that. What about socialization? Those kids never got out of the house except to go to church almost every day of the week. Which brought up another point: When *was* education going on? Eliza didn't even have a teaching degree, so how could she teach their son in junior high? No, I certainly wasn't going down that road. I wasn't *that* desperate. Besides, I loved our public school system. I was involved as I could be and used most of my vacation days to be at classroom parties and school functions.

Homeschooling wasn't an option. I knew there was no

way I would have the patience or the knowledge to teach my own children. Then Saturday, March twenty-third happened.

I had an epiphany of sorts. I was in the kitchen drilling my third-grader on multiplication facts, watching my first-grader blend letter clusters, and helping my fourth-grader write a report that was due Monday. Somewhere between correcting spelling, finding a topic sentence, skip-counting a song about the multiples of eights, and sounding out c-l-o-c-k, it hit me: *I'm home-schooling—and I love it!*

This moment stayed with me and would not go away for the rest of the school year. During that time I became increasingly frustrated with the level of stress in our home. I was yelling at the kids every morning, they were fighting about anything and everything, and I hadn't been on a date with Ted since Christmas vacation. It was time to ask myself the hard questions.

It suddenly hit me: I'm homeschooling—and I love it!

I invited Eliza to meet me for a latte and was surprised when she didn't hesitate—I figured she probably *never* had a free moment. I was somewhat hesitant to open up to her because snobbery can go both ways. It was my impression of homeschoolers that they had a superior attitude, especially towards public school. My feeling was, *Don't tell me the negatives of public school, especially if your children have never been in public school.* But I really did want to know how homeschooling had been beneficial for her family—and how she found time to do it.

Eliza proceeded to tell me just that. As she talked, I

realized that I had judged her without really looking beyond my stereotype of homeschoolers. She answered many of the questions I had and calmed even more of my fears. For one thing, the reason she was able to meet me for coffee was because her children were at a church-sponsored youth function. Ironically, my complaint about them always being at church negated my question about socialization. They had tons of friends at church and spent plenty of time interacting with other kids.

Eliza graciously brought along one of her children's portfolios to show what the kids were learning and how they were doing it. As I looked through the reports, poems, hypotheses and subsequent discoveries, and math worksheets, I realized that they were somehow getting plenty of work done. Eliza explained that school just didn't take that much time when you eliminated roll call, time between classes, thirty kids handing in assignments, recess, announcements, and so forth, so their family often finished school by noon. Wow!

What touched me the most was when Eliza said, "I have always heard parents of adult children say, 'They grow up so fast' and 'Enjoy them while they are young because they won't stay that way for long.' With comments like that, I thought I should homeschool so that I can enjoy and be a part of that brief, precious time."

It's funny, but I remembered on Hunter's first day of kindergarten thinking, *Why am I sending him off now just when he's getting really fun to be around?* As he got older I thought, *And why does the school get the best part of his day, and I get the dregs when he's tired and cranky and I have to force him to do hours of homework? They have him for seven hours—why can't they get all the work done in that amount of time?*

The clincher for me happened the following month, at the end-of-the-year party for Hunter's class. The school principal told us parents to enjoy our fourth-graders this summer because it would never be the same again. He predicted that in fifth grade we would lose our children to society and recommended we prepare for a roller coaster ride over the next two years. We were told that right now our children will defend their parents because they know we are right, but within the year they will be arguing with their parents and defending their friends.

I walked out of that classroom thinking, *I don't have to do this; I have an alternative.* Now that I think about it, I probably should have thanked that gentleman for leading me in the right direction. The next question was, now that I know where I'm going, how am I going to get there? What about my career?

WHAT AM I REALLY WORKING FOR?

It was time that I slowed down a little and took a look under the hood. Why was I working in the first place? For one thing, I enjoyed my work. It fulfilled something in me that motherhood alone didn't—I had a sense of accomplishment. At the office I could work hard, do a good job, get paid for it, receive some affirmation, check it off, and move on.

At home, no matter how hard I worked, I never felt like I accomplished anything. I would clean the kitchen, only to turn around and find a dirty glass in the sink. Just as I was folding the last pair of pants, another pair was being tossed in the hamper. About the time we nipped whining in the bud, sassing started. If I became a stay-at-home mom, would I ever feel productive again?

And I'll be honest with you, there were many mornings I couldn't wait to get out of that house so I could enjoy the peace and quiet of the work environment. I looked forward to lunch with the girls, conversation with grown-ups, and office parties. People thought I was funny, intelligent, and stimulating. I felt appreciated—something I didn't feel at home.

But the bottom line was money; we needed the second income. The money that I made allowed us to live a little more comfortably. Then the thought hit me, *How much am I actually adding to the monthly budget?* I don't know why I had never stopped to really calculate the difference I was making, or not making.

I took my net monthly salary and subtracted the money spent on gasoline to drive to work everyday. I didn't bother calculating mileage and wear and tear on the car, although I knew that, too, would make a difference. I figured my car insurance would go down since my car would be considered a leisure vehicle instead of a commuter car. Then I deducted a big chunk of change representing the money I spent on shopping every month to dress for success. That plus the exorbitant dry cleaning bills knocked the total down quite a bit.

Those much-loved lunches with the girls every day sure did add up. Good thing I had never stopped to figure it out, or I might have lost my appetite. The fun-filled office parties weren't quite so fun once I made some quick tabulations of how much I was spending on gifts regularly.

Oops, another biggie. Food. All those quick-fix meals in a box, frozen foods, and fast food—convenience comes at a cost. Then there were the prepackaged Lunchables for the kids at three bucks a pop when I was in too much of a hurry to make PB&J for their lunches. And I hadn't even added in the cost of those special times when our family gathered around the table for a meal, usually at a restaurant.

Was there going to be any money left? Not much. And as Ted pointed out, my income knocked us into a higher tax bracket, so it was even costing *him* for me to work. I was very surprised at Ted's reaction when I showed him these numbers and told him what I was considering: He was excited! I thought all along that he wanted me to work because it helped take some of the pressure off of him. He couldn't *wait* for me to come home.

COMING HOME

We got a babysitter one night and went out to dinner to come up with a plan to make it happen. Ted's first question was how much was homeschooling going to cost. Eliza told me that it could cost as much or as little as you had to spend, but the average was around three hundred dollars per child. But as I pointed out to Ted, you would be amazed at how much we pour into the "free" school system when you sit down to add up the money that we sent with the kids for this project or that fund-raiser or this activity or that field trip. Then there was lunch money and snack money. It certainly didn't cost as much as we were spending on day care every month before they went to school, but it wasn't cheap either.

Over dessert we summed up our plan. I would give my notice right away so I could spend the summer with the kids. (That saved us a few more dollars on summer day care and camp programs.) We decided to pull back on some of the kid's extracurricular activities to pay for the homeschool supplies, with an eye toward looking into some of the local parks-and-recreation sports leagues and activities.

Ted and I were so giddy that we couldn't wait to come home and tell the kids. Boy, that was a shocker: They were less than enthusiastic about being homeschooled.

My children loved the idea of me not working outside the home, but they weren't so sure about leaving their friends at school. However, summer vacation had a way of warming them up to the idea, so by fall they were willing to give it a shot.

THE PRINCIPLE APPROACH:
BUILDING A MORAL FOUNDATION

By this time I had zeroed in on the *principle approach* to homeschooling. My choice was a surprise to everyone, including me. You see, I was not a particularly religious person and this is a distinctly Christian approach to learning. What attracted me to it was the idea that our country and its government were founded on strong moral principles, specifically biblical principles. In these principles our founding fathers discovered the strength and courage to pursue liberty at great personal risk. They believed in something enough to die for it. I was drawn to the idea of raising children with that kind of passion and courage.

The principle approach focuses on providential history, the belief that God has had a hand in everything from the beginning and that His work didn't stop at the final book of the Bible. In other words, history is "His story." From this basic premise, we study every subject to see how all of the pieces of history and knowledge come together to answer this one question: What has God been up to and why? This approach to learning has really captured the imaginations of our children, and it shows in the quality of their schoolwork.

In the course of learning about our nation's heritage, they are doing a lot of writing. This approach requires the children to write essays about what they have learned, and from what I read I know whether they have really understood the teaching. I can evaluate their mastery of grammar, punctuation, and spelling in context and not based on their ability to fill in the blanks of a dry workbook page. And the kids are learning so much from their own writing!

Language arts, history, and geography are all covered in this format. Currently, we are doing math and science using more traditional textbooks, but as we all become more experienced, I might look into using the principle approach to teach some of the other subjects.

It's A Miracle!

Looking at our own little family timeline, I can certainly see how the hand of Providence has led us to this moment. Despite my bias against homeschooling, we were led to give it a try. And little by little, God has drawn our family back together, with everyone looking in the same direction—toward Him. As we study the lives of individuals in history in the light of His eternal plan, we are beginning to believe that we, too, each have a purpose greater than living for ourselves. I must admit that when I left the office and came home, I didn't expect to find God there.

As you can see, homeschooling has been nothing short of miraculous for us. I cannot even begin to describe the change that has come over our family. And I love being a stay-at-home mom! I'm more relaxed, and I don't yell at the kids so much. We now often gather around our own kitchen table for home-cooked family meals. We dusted off the croquet set from the attic for playing together on warm nights, and we pull out the Monopoly game for chilly ones.

One of the things I was worried about was that the kids would fight all day. I don't know if it's because I'm more peaceful or because they are together all day and have gotten to know each other better. But whatever it is, the kids are definitely closer than they've ever been. I have grown closer to them, too. Time to get to know your kids is a luxury of inestimable value.

But I've noticed the biggest change in Ted. He walks around like a kid with a secret. He comes home from work earlier. We all go to bed at the same time now. And Ted and I get up at the crack of dawn so we can have some quiet time together.

He bought me my own caffe latte machine for my birthday with a card that read, "Meet me in the kitchen every morning before the kids wake up. We have a 'latte' to talk about." And we do. Our relationship has grown so much now that I'm not spread so thin. I came home to spend more time with my children and ended up becoming best friends with my husband. Who would have guessed that homeschooling could be good for your marriage?

If I've learned one thing, it is this: Homeschooling is as much about *home* as it is about *schooling*.

Chapter Four

I'm No Super Mom

Come on in, the door is open. Pardon me for not getting up; I'm not having one of my better days. I'm sorry—just move those magazines and have a seat on the sofa. No, you're not interrupting anything. I was just grading some papers, which I don't mind setting aside, and the girls are on the computer in the family room. On days like this, we supplement their assignments with educational software. Thankfully, I was feeling better yesterday, so we were able to work ahead a bit in the lesson plan.

So you want to know if homeschooling is the best option for your family. I would love to be able to offer you fresh-baked cookies and my best Donna Reed smile and say, "You can do it, too, no problem!" But that wouldn't really be fair to you.

DON'T TELL ME ABOUT YOUR PERFECT LIFE

First of all, you should know that there is no such thing as the perfect homeschooling family—just like there are excellent public schoolteachers and those who should have retired ten years ago. Of course, homeschooling presents its own special challenges for a mother with chronic fatigue immune deficiency syndrome. I have good days when I feel strong and filled with wisdom and patience; then there are the bad days when I wake up exhausted and grumpy and I can only lie on the couch and teach with a dry erase board. I guess ours won't be chosen as a poster family for homeschooling anytime soon, but I truly love teaching our children at home and wouldn't have it any other way.

Besides, if you're anything like me, hearing about a Super-Mom educating her little Einsteins would convince you quicker than anything that you're not cut out for this job. Maybe in your research you've read magazine articles that go something like this:

> While Junior prepares for his meeting with the mayor to discuss community service opportunities for local youth, I grind wheat harvested from the back forty to make fresh pasta for dinner while helping my kindergartener memorize the periodic table of elements. My oldest daughter hand-stitches the final square on the quilt she is entering in the county fair after helping her little sister learn to read—in French. Thankfully, my toddler is content in the other room building a working windmill out of clothespins. We can't wait for Papa to return home from his mission trip so we can tell him the good news: Bubba scored a perfect 1600 on his SATs; Sissy won the Our Little Miss Perfect pageant; Junior is the youngest

child ever to win the International Latin Spelling Bee; and little Bubba Jr. potty trained himself because he wanted to honor his parents.

Talk about intimidating! I'm happy if at the end of the day we've at least completed the requisite math and language arts, the girls are still speaking to each other, and I'm the recipient of a voluntary hug before bedtime. There was a time when even that was too much to hope for.

Rebellion and Relationships: A Study in Contrasts

When my daughters were young, they were best friends. They would play with their Barbies together for hours, brush each other's hair, and sneak into the same bed at night. But after they started school, I noticed them slowly begin to grow apart. At first I told myself that it was good for them to develop some individuality.

However, when Kristen, my oldest, hit her middle school years, she suddenly didn't want anything to do with her family at all! Again, I figured it was just part of growing up, the natural progression from parental dependence to peer support. But over time she began to show an obvious disdain for me as well as an outright defiance of her father. I could never imagine talking to *my* mother the way Kristen talked to me.

What was I doing wrong? I tried to be her friend, but she only mouthed off more. Her father laid down the law and came down hard on Kristen when she disobeyed— which yielded further rebellion. The way her friends dressed scared me. I later learned that she was changing into clothes borrowed from her friends and heaping on makeup once she got to school. Not only was I appalled, but I frankly felt sorry for the boys at school. How could they be expected to keep their minds on studying with all that bare flesh dancing around in front of them?

I know I sound like an old fuddy-duddy. But I tried being the hip, cool mom, and that only embarrassed my daughter more. I was losing touch with her just as surely as the world was reaching out for her. My only hope was that this was just a teenage phase and it would pass.

Meanwhile, it was breaking my heart to watch the way Kristen treated her little sister. I don't think she *ever* had a kind word to say to Chelsea. The gap between the girls grew wider every day, the animosity reaching a fevered pitch every afternoon on the drive home from school. The nonstop bickering was killing me, and many times I would call my husband and ask him to pick up the girls just because I knew I wouldn't be able to deal with it.

How Shopping Changed My Life

Then one day I ran into a family at the mall—an encounter that changed my life. At first glance, I thought it was odd to see so many children out of school in the middle of the day. Then I noticed that they all had clipboards in their hands. Intrigued by their enthusiasm and boldness, I stood and watched these charming children for more than thirty minutes. I was mesmerized as they randomly interviewed strangers and asked them what Christmas meant to their families and what traditions they were passing down to the next generation.

There were three or four children carrying on various conversations, while their mother sat nearby watching and feeding Cheerios to a toddler. The older children took turns helping to entertain the little boy when he tired of eating cereal and began sticking O's in every orifice of his body and in the hair of his baby sister sleeping in the stroller.

Eventually I was spotted by an adorable teenage girl, who made a beeline for me with her clipboard at the ready. She was extremely polite and considerate, asking to make sure she wasn't interrupting my shopping time. I was impressed by the way she looked me directly in the eyes and genuinely appreciated my answers.

I had to find out more about these children, so I went over and sat down beside their mother. I instantly understood who deserved the credit for these kids. She gave me the sweetest smile and a sincere "Merry Christmas!" This woman was so open that I felt comfortable asking about her children. She explained to me that they had been homeschooled all their lives.

I had heard of homeschooling and even knew of a few families in our neighborhood who did it. I wanted to know more, so I turned the tables on these little "market researchers" and began asking *them* questions. I was blown away by their articulate answers and obvious love for one another. By the time I had to rush off to pick up the girls from school, this family had left an indelible mark on me.

HONEY, LET'S HOMESCHOOL!

I couldn't wait to tell my husband about my discovery. I just knew that homeschooling was the answer for our family.

So I was deflated and disappointed when Sydney said he was completely opposed to the idea. Nothing I could say was going to change his mind. I must give Sydney credit—I know he was only looking out for me. He was worried that the stress would be too much in my condition. He also expressed concern that I would not be able to adequately prepare them for college.

I had learned from experience not to argue with my husband. Even if I ultimately won, I always lost more in the victory than if I had simply trusted him in the first place. Besides, I knew I couldn't take on something of this magnitude without his support. I had voiced my opinion and that was all I could do.

Well, maybe not all. I did tell God that if He wanted me to homeschool my daughters then He would need to change Sydney's mind. In the meantime, I just *happened* to leave some statistics by his favorite reading chair (in the bathroom). I thought he should know that the average homeschooled child scored 87 percent on standardized tests, compared to the average public school student who scored 50 percent.

I just knew that homeschooling was the answer for our family.

True, instead of a college degree, I had only an Mrs. degree (which I received after my junior year of college); but I found some more interesting numbers. Homeschool children whose mothers had little more than a smattering of education beyond high school scored nearly as high as kids whose mothers had a college degree or teaching credentials! Not bad, huh?

Unfortunately, Sydney wasn't buying.

BUSTED

Thankfully, things improved tremendously around our house over the Christmas vacation. Within days the "old Kristen" we knew and loved had seemingly returned. She and Chelsea had so much fun together decorating the tree, baking cookies, and creating homemade ornaments. Kristen even spent her own money to buy Chelsea a locket. It was a Christmas miracle.

Sadly, this peace on earth was short-lived. As soon as Kristen returned to school, I didn't recognize her anymore. And it was almost more than I could take when a similar attitude began sneaking into *Chelsea's* tone of voice. I knew that I had done my absolute best to teach my girls how to be kind and respectful, but it is hard to compete with the world's influence when your child is away from you eight hours a day. Inevitably, they are going to be shaped most by those they spend the most time with. I was tempted to simply give up.

Then one night Sydney was helping Chelsea with her homework. He was looking through some of her answers and realized that none of them had anything to do with the questions being asked. When challenged she nonchalantly responded, "Oh Dad, it's okay; they only check to make sure you have something written in the blanks." As Sydney probed deeper, he realized that Chelsea had been "faking it" for a long time. She could barely read or spell at her grade level, and yet she had been receiving passing grades every semester.

The very next day, Sydney learned through a coworker that his daughter and our Chelsea had been caught in the school bathroom hanging with two other girls who had marijuana in their pockets. The two with the pot were expelled, but Chelsea and the other girl were let off with a warning from the principal to "be more careful with whom you hang around." And he promised not to tell their parents.

My husband came home irate. How dare the school not tell us that our nine-year-old was found even in the same room with drugs! When we confronted Chelsea, the dam broke loose and we discovered that all the rejection she had been internalizing from her big sister was being magnified by her inability to penetrate the all-powerful fourth grade girl cliques. It scared Sydney to think that Chelsea was so hungry for approval that she might fall in with the wrong crowd to gain acceptance.

That night Sydney and I stayed up talking past midnight. We decided to let the girls finish out the school year, but he agreed we should try homeschooling them the following year. Even after determining that he would share the teaching responsibilities, Sydney was still hesitant because of my health. I promised that we could reevaluate at the end of each school year to determine whether to continue or not. If at any point we felt like the girls were failing academically, or more importantly, if he felt like I was failing physically, then we would send them back to school.

TRADITIONAL TEXTS: HOMESCHOOLING BY THE BOOK

I spent that summer combing through homeschool resource books, magazines, and the Internet for information. We decided that the best curriculum for our situation was a traditional textbook package. That way Sydney could feel confident that the girls were staying on track and could, if necessary, easily reenter public school at their regular grade level.

Fortunately, it doesn't look like that will be necessary. We've been homeschooling for almost a year now, and it couldn't be going better. At first, Kristen hated the idea of not going to public school. We assured her that we would approach this on a year-to-year basis. Everyone's opinion and feelings would be considered when deciding how long we would try this experiment. Our first year isn't over yet, but no one in the family seems hesitant about continuing this indefinitely. So far, so good.

Using traditional textbooks has proven to be perfect for our situation. Before going to work, Sydney teaches any new concepts and answers any particularly tough questions from the day before. As it turns out, the girls are able to understand most of the instruction themselves with little supervision. Not that it's a problem when they do need my help in the middle of the day. When in doubt, I simply reach for my handy-dandy teacher's manual and get it straight in my own mind before showing the girls what they are missing. I usually end up spending about two hours with each daughter, overseeing their work. Kristen is able to check her own work, but I often help Sydney by grading Chelsea's assignments. Homeschool for us is truly a family affair!

Because the textbooks are divided into daily lesson plans, we are able to assign a week's worth of work to each girl on Monday. They know they can approach it any way they choose, as long as all of the work is completed by

Friday. It's fun to watch the girls develop their own personal organizational styles. Kristen tackles her hardest subjects first—math and science—and then breezes through the rest of the week with the remaining subjects. Chelsea, on the other hand, likes to balance out her workload over a four-day period. That way if something comes up during the week, or if I'm having a particularly hard day, she has a day "in the bank" that she can fall back on.

Someone wisely recommended that we not try to teach every possible subject or even everything that is in each textbook. Even so, the girls are growing in real understanding by leaps and bounds. I love watching the light bulb switch on when they really get something Sydney or I are teaching.

The most priceless moments are when I'm watching my girls and they don't know it. Their very countenance has changed—they somehow seem younger, but in a good way. Kristen spends hours curled up on the couch reading a book in a cozy warm-up suit. I can tell she feels much more comfortable remaining a little girl for just a few more years. I don't know what she did with the makeup she had stashed; I haven't asked.

Sydney is thrilled with the education the girls are receiving. And you can't imagine what it does to this mother's heart to see my daughters becoming best friends again. More than a few times I've awakened from a nap to find Kristen helping Chelsea with her schoolwork. I wouldn't tell Sydney this, but if they hadn't learned one thing all year long, homeschooling would still be worth it to me just to see that.

We may have begun homeschooling because of peer

pressure, substandard education, and the bad attitudes our girls were picking up in school. But what will keep us homeschooling are things like seeing the girls rediscover the joy of learning, the rebuilding of family relationships, and having the privilege of once again being the primary influence in our children's lives.

Chapter Five

My Dad's Secret Identity

You couldn't have chosen a better time to visit. Now is the lull before the storm. Not that Monica's arrival is akin to a hurricane, but the atmosphere certainly does change when my wife gets home. There's no one quite like a mother in a child's life, is there?

Anyway, have a seat. We should be able to catch a few minutes of uninterrupted conversation. Savannah is at art class, Clarissa is upstairs reading, and Tristyn is hanging out in the cul-de-sac with his buddies. I should be working on my dissertation, but I would much rather talk about homeschooling.

I would guess that you haven't run across too many homeschooling families where the father is the primary teacher. Am I right? There are more of us than you might imagine, but we're a little less visible because we don't usually hang out at co-ops or tea talks with the other mothers. I can't ever seem to find a thing to wear that doesn't make me look fat, so I just don't go! Seriously though, I really don't fit in.

So what else is new? From the day Monica and I were

married, we've been shocking our relatives. For the first few years, I worked as a finish carpenter to put her through medical school. Now that she is established in her own practice, I have returned to graduate school, taking night classes to earn my PhD.

But by day, I'm Teacher Dad!

THE MOTHER OF ALL TEACHERS

That doesn't mean I'm in this alone. Although I'm in charge of the core academic subjects, Monica is very involved with the kids, teaching them Latin and imparting basic life skills. I don't know what I'd do without her help.

Because she is gone much of the day and many evenings, Monica insists on assuming responsibility for the morning and late night shifts. The day begins when she wakes the kids with her silly "Good Morning, Toadstools" song, sung operatic-style in full Wagnerian soprano. She is great about gathering the kids into the kitchen to prepare a hearty breakfast, drawing out insightful conversation, instigating healthy debate, and making sure they realize the importance of laughter.

Monica also oversees the bedtime ritual, which includes discussions in the dark at the edge of the bed. She particularly loves bedtime because she has discovered that the kids' hearts are more readily opened, and thus more easily seen, with the lights out. Being both a night owl and an early bird, I am able to get much of my doctoral thesis research done at these times.

Many people find it hard to believe that although the majority of my day is spent investing in my children's education, I don't feel like less of a man. Believe it or not, molding young lives, filling their minds, and shaping their hearts does wonders for the ego. Watching my students assimilate information, organize it logically, and apply it with wisdom is quantifiably productive and extremely rewarding.

Of course, I've tried explaining this to my in-laws, but they remain less than supportive of our homeschooling efforts. When we first announced that we were thinking about homeschooling, I believe the term they used was "moronic." Of course, the first grenade they always lob in our direction is the issue of socialization. My first line of defense is to define the question: "Do you mean opportunities to socialize or socialization?" If they mean the former, then that's easy. Between art classes, chess club, playing with the neighbor kids, sleepovers, soccer, and summer camp, we've got the whole social outlet thing covered.

Now if they are referring to true socialization, then I have to admit that I'm not too eager to see my kids *socialized*. Dictionary.com cites three definitions for the word:

1. To place under government or group ownership or control.
2. To make fit for companionship with others; make sociable.
3. To convert or adapt to the needs of society.

Let's see. Number one, nope. I don't think so. Number two, I present exhibits A, B, and C: Savannah, Clarissa, and Tristyn, three of the most enjoyable companions with whom I'd ever want to socialize. Number three, I'm sorry, but have you taken a look at society lately? I'm not interested in seeing my children either convert *or* adapt to what passes for the needs of society these days.

I'm not ashamed to admit that my educational goals for them do not include making sure my children fit into society. Because it has been my experience that children reach the level of expectation you have for them, I have set a higher standard for our family—not only socially, but academically as well.

I remember, as a child in school, taking open-book tests. Quizzes would cover the text word for word. All I was required to do was to skim through the chapter until I found the sentence in question and fill in the blank. I just wanted to pass the test and get on to the next book so that eventually I could get on with real life. I was just marking time in school, waiting for life to begin. I don't want that for my kids. I want them to be thrilled about life *now* and to be prepared for what lies ahead.

I have set a higher standard for our family—not only socially, but academically as well.

I believe that I'm the best teacher for my children—not because I'm earning a doctorate, but because there is nobody in this world who cares more about our children's future than Monica and me. My father always told me, "If you want something done right, then do it yourself." That's why I am the best teacher for my children. For one thing, I know them so well. The more time I spend with them, the better I understand them and the more superior education I can give them. You really can't dispute the benefits of a teacher-student ratio of one-to-one, or even one-to-three.

True, I'm a horrible speller and math is my Achilles'

heel. But my lack of expertise in those areas doesn't disqualify me from being able to teach those subjects. Hey, if I don't remember how to do an advanced calculus equation, I'll either learn how or find somebody who knows. And thank heaven for spell-check!

Homeschooling provides an opportunity for a superior education for a variety of reasons. Allowing children to work at their own pace is reason enough. Think of all the children in public school who don't have the chance to master one skill before having to rush on to the next one. We all know that much of learning is building upon that which we already know. What would it feel like not to know the first step? From that point on, you would always be trying to catch up—while making sure nobody ever figured out that you were behind.

Then there's the other extreme, the quick student who learns early on that school is boring. What a shame to have bright minds dulled by the restraints inherent in a classroom situation where a teacher has to herd thirty students in the same direction at the same time.

Okay, I had better get down off of my soapbox before Clarissa finishes her book and discovers we're having a party in here. I might not get the opportunity to tell you about my real passion, *classical education.*

CLASSICAL EDUCATION:
THERE'S NO PLACE LIKE ROME

When I first discovered the classical approach to homeschooling, I found that it summed up everything I instinctively knew I wanted to teach my children without knowing exactly how to impart that knowledge. This method of teaching is not only classical because it was the way children were taught in ancient Greece and Rome, but also because it provides the kind of education that stands the test of time.

Okay, bear with me while I attempt to describe a rather complicated teaching method without the benefit of modern-day language. Classic learning revolves around an ancient pedagogical concept called the *trivium*. The trivium, which means "three roads," consists of three distinct periods of instruction that parallel the three cognitive developmental phases of childhood. In other words, we teach our children what their minds are geared for learning at different stages of growth.

For instance, Tristyn, my nine-year-old son, is in the *grammar* stage of learning. I don't mean grammar as in diagramming sentences; I'm talking about fundamental principles. From the time Tristyn could talk, we've been filling him with bits of knowledge. Children in this stage are sponges for information. They may not know how to process all of it, but they certainly can absorb it by the bucketful. We are taking advantage of this window of time to teach him math facts, spelling rules, historical dates, foreign languages, states and capitals, Scripture verses, and phonics. We have a lot of fun with mnemonics, too. Kids spend a great deal of time memorizing facts during the grammar stage.

By the time a child reaches the next stage—the *dialectic*, or logic, phase—he is more than ready to put those facts to good use. Clarissa, our twelve-year-old daughter, is now discovering the excitement of moving from the "what" of the grammar phase to the "why" and "how" of the dialectic. That is, she is taking the concrete information she has gathered previously and learning to think about it analytically.

For instance, while in the grammar stage, Clarissa learned that the Declaration of Independence was signed on July 4, 1776. Now in the dialectic phase, we are discussing *why* the colonies sought liberation from Great Britain and *how* they made it happen. And Clarissa hasn't gone so far as to thank me yet, but I think she is beginning to understand why I subjected her to timed math drills every day for the first few school years. It sure makes computing and calculating much easier when you don't have to stop and think to remember your math facts.

The final stage of learning, the *rhetoric* phase, is my favorite. Savannah, our sixteen-year-old, is enjoying the fruit of many hours of hard work and self-discipline. At this point she could gain entrance to the finest of colleges. Instead, she is taking the next two years to pursue the areas of study she enjoys most. For example, she loves the arts. I mean art appreciation in its broader context, not simply oil painting or playing the piano. (Although I don't think I'm just being a proud papa when I say that she is gifted in both of these areas.) Show her any famous painting, and she can name the artist and the period. Same goes for any piece of classical music.

Don't misunderstand me—I continue to assign Savannah schoolwork. She is required (not that she doesn't love it) to spend many hours a day reading great works of literature. I am a big believer in continuing education, and I can think of no greater instructor than a good book. I agree with Thomas Carlyle, the British historian, who said,

"What we become depends on what we read after all the professors have finished with us. The greatest university of all is the collection of books."

For me, the most enjoyable and fulfilling part of the rhetoric stage is the focus on self-expression. Monica and I encourage Clarissa toward passionate debate, respectful opinions, and persuasive writing. My goal has been to fill her mind with solid facts, then train her to think for herself. And now we have the pleasure of watching her unfurl her sails as she confidently sets out to navigate the world before her.

Let any man try and tell me that climbing the corporate ladder is more fulfilling than that.

Chapter Six

It's Not Just an Education— It's an Adventure

Ciao! Come on in. No, I'm not Italian. My husband was stationed in Naples when we first got married, and I tend to pick up one or two things from every place we live. You should come by to sample my Cajun cooking sometime. I even learned how to tap a maple tree to make syrup—although that particular skill doesn't come in very handy here.

Pardon the mess. I would love to offer up a great excuse—a tornado, a riot, a marauding pack of wolves—but the truth is our house looks like this most of the time. I have resigned myself to the fact that I can't do it all. Something has to give, and it usually ends up being the house or my appearance or both. This morning I chose to put on makeup and get out of my pajamas since we were having company.

It gets really tricky when my husband, Carlos, returns home and I have to pull myself and the house together on the same day. He spends seven to ten days at sea, and then he's home for twenty-four to forty-eight hours. As you can tell by the empty frozen food boxes from lunch, he's away this week.

This is real life. I don't know about the other homes you've visited, but you can consider mine a reality check. Let me start by assuring you that I love homeschooling and count it a privilege to live in a time when the practice is so acceptable and the resources so accessible. That said, allow me to let you in on a few secrets that I wish someone would have shared with me when I was first thinking about homeschooling.

First of all, don't believe everything you read in the homeschooling books. Remember, they are usually trying to put their best face forward to convince you that home-schooling is the perfect option for every family. I agree with them in theory; but every once in a while I wish they would portray a normal family with average kids, a father who is not at all involved in the actual homeschooling, and a mother who feels like pulling her hair out much of the time.

Secondly, I wish someone would have warned me about burnout. This usually hits when I'm trying to do all the things the homeschool books, magazines, and Internet sites say I should be doing. The problem is, I try to incorporate all of these great ideas at once, forgetting that these suggestions are coming from multiple families talking about their *best* days.

Thankfully, I've learned that when I'm having one of those "I'm a failure and my kids would be better off at a real school" mornings, I need to look for a change of pace. Sometimes we'll go for a bicycle ride and call it P.E., or spend a day in the kitchen and call it Home Ec, or go shopping and call it Math (mostly subtraction). If all else fails, I buy the biggest bar of chocolate I can find and call it Health 101.

And another thing: I'm sorry, but my kids don't always like school. There are plenty of mornings when they whine, complain, and argue about having to do their work. One of my standard lines is "Would you be acting like this if you were standing in front of thirty other kids with a principal just down the hall?" The fact is, I am first and foremost Mom, and it's hard for all of us to switch gears sometimes. In that case, if they don't obey Teacher Mom, then they have to face Mother Mom, and she controls the phone privileges and television remote and sleepover permissions.

Lastly, you can ignore the whole socialization controversy. It's a non-issue. I like the Mary Beth Nelsen quote that's popular among homeschoolers. When asked if socialization was a problem for her family, she answered, "We did tend to oversocialize when we first started homeschooling, but I think we have it under control now."[1] We spend so much time on the go between co-op classes, play rehearsals, volleyball practice, and other activities that I'm tempted to call what we do "minivan-schooling." The only problem with socialization is staying home enough to get the schooling done.

Okay, with all that out on the table, let me reiterate what I stated at the very beginning: I love homeschooling. Do I get tired? Do I get jealous of the other military moms who have six hours a day to fix their face, their hair, their plumbing, and their dinner? Do I get really impatient when my youngest daughter just doesn't get it after

I've explained it fifteen different ways? Yes, yes, and you bet. But is it worth it? A thousand times yes!

Homeschooling is perfect for our family for a number of reasons, but two in particular stand out above the rest. The first one is probably pretty obvious: We have moved seven times in the last twenty years. I personally love exciting new adventures, but our oldest daughter, Carmelita, did not inherit my temperament. She was enrolled in the DoD schools—oh, pardon me. I forgot I'm talking to civilians. DoD stands for the Department of Defense, which operates schools on the naval bases. Anyway, Carmelita loved school and did very well; but every time we moved, it would throw her into a tailspin, complete with anxiety attacks. She doesn't even like to have the *furniture in her room rearranged.* This was a problem, considering her father is career military.

The year she was to begin junior high, we received our next PCS (Permanent Change of Station) orders. Our next-door neighbor, who had befriended Carmelita, recommended homeschooling. At first I thought she was wacky, until I looked into it further. Then I thought I was the wacky one and wondered why I hadn't thought of it first. It was perfect. We had been given several options of *where* to move, so I got on the Web and checked out the homeschooling laws in each potential state, and we factored these into our decision.

Homeschooling has made all the difference in subsequent moves. Carmelita doesn't have to switch gears with every new teacher and school district. No more trying to fit in or figure out what was acceptable or cause for ridicule, cool and not cool—or jostling around until she finds her "rank" in the DoD school pecking order.

Best of all, we've said goodbye to learning gaps! It was frustrating for all of us to transfer to a new duty station, only to discover that Carmelita's new class had already learned some fundamental new step in math or grammar and she was behind before she even started. Now all we have to do is pack up our homeschool supplies, take a cross-country trip, unpack, and pick up right where we left off. Same teacher, same students, same curriculum. The children have actually enjoyed the last couple of moves!

And we've learned to include the PCS moves as part of our homeschooling. We've discovered that the best part is getting there. The long stretches of highway provide for leisurely conversation, which is a stolen treasure these days. If possible, we take a week or two to get where we're going, stopping along the way to smell the roses, the pine trees, the bison patties, the ocean spray, or any other of the fabulous scents America has to offer. There's not a state in the union that won't let you count the trip as school if you make a couple of "educational" stops along the way. Do you have any idea how many monuments, historical landmarks, and rinky-dink but fascinating museums there are in just about every town you drive through? Homeschooling has put the adventure back into military life.

KNOW YOUR LEARNING STYLES: DIFFERENT KIDS, DIFFERENT METHODS

The other reason we know that homeschooling is the right choice for our family is the superior education that I can offer my children. Not because I'm so smart, but simply because I know my children and I know how they learn best. There is no way a schoolteacher can adjust her teaching style twenty-five times a day to meet the needs of everyone in her class. But I can for three. I can give my children the individualized time, teaching, and learning tools they need.

My nine-year-old daughter, Elena, is a bundle of living sunshine. She is constantly skipping, singing, giggling, hugging, and drawing—sometimes all at once. Because I can embrace her enthusiasm instead of having to squelch it to maintain order in a classroom, I can tap into this energy to help her learn. Elena would probably be classified as an auditory/kinesthetic learner with the auditory modal becoming more dominant as she gets older. What this means to me as her teacher is that if I can find a way to feed information to her through auditory means, she is going to be able to assimilate it more thoroughly and completely. Effective learning tools for her include audiotapes, oral book reports, discussion, reading aloud, and perhaps most effective, singing. For instance, I could give Elena a sheet of multiplication facts to memorize and she could study them all day long and never be able to remember them. But if I teach her a counting song, she can have her times tables down cold before I even teach her how to multiply.

Okay, a funny story. My in-laws were not pro-homeschooling and often asked us when we'd be putting the children back into "the system." They were visiting for Thanksgiving and we were cleaning up the kitchen with Carlos' mother, Olivia, when Elena started singing some geography songs. Slowly my mother-in-law realized what she was singing: "Belize, Canada, Costa Rica, to name a few; El Salvador, Honduras, Mexico, Old not New; Guatemala, Nicaragua, and good ole USA! These are the North American countries—let me show the way." Olivia's eyes about popped out of her head! When she recovered she asked Elena, "Yes, but do you know where those places are?" Elena replied, "Sure, Grandma, don't you know? Come look at the map and I'll teach you."

Soon my eleven-year-old son, Nicolas, who has to be in the middle of everything, joined in the act and started singing his ABC's. Grandma sat down and with tears in her eyes looked in mine and said, "Will you forgive me?" Sound overly dramatic to you? It wouldn't if you knew Nicolas. You see, Niko is severely learning-disabled.

I have only been homeschooling him for a couple of years. At first I didn't think I could do it, even though my other two were thriving at home. I assumed that the professionals could do a better job with him. I was wrong. They knew their jobs better than I did, but they didn't know my son better.

When he was in school, he spoke only in grunts and phrases. Since I've been working with him, Niko speaks in complete sentences, sings his ABC's, counts his Matchbox cars, and is even learning his vowel sounds. Remarkable teacher? No. Remarkable son? Yes. Only it took a mother's love to find him.

I can give my children the individualized time, teaching, and learning tools they need.

I discovered that Niko is what is known as a tactile/kinesthetic learner, meaning that sometimes he needs to use his whole body to learn something. For example, we are working on counting using a big hopscotch grid I've outlined in tape on the basement floor. Niko hops to the number one and we say "One!" together. Then he jumps one more block to the two and we say "Two!" together.

Other times, he likes to feel things with his hands. A plastic tub filled with warm water next to a plastic tub filled with cold water helped Niko to understand the difference between warm and cold. And when he works his puzzles, he likes to feel the outline of the piece and the place where it goes. Somehow, seeing it and feeling it helps him to process the information more effectively.

He's still in speech and occupational therapy, and I still must determine every morning whether he is having a good day or a bad day and how much we should try to accomplish that day. Niko can't sit in a chair for longer than thirty minutes, so I often work with him by teaching him how to cook. He wants to be by my side, or anybody else's, every minute of the day. He is extremely social, so I've learned to incorporate that gift into his teaching.

When I'm working with Elena, Niko joins us and practices his motor skills by cutting and pasting and coloring. He's a master at puzzles and he loves rewards. So to find some extra time to teach my other two children, I've worked out a deal with Niko. For every puzzle he finishes, he gets to pick a jelly bean out of the jar we keep on top of the bread box. But he can only eat it after he's identified what color it is. Even still, his is the biggest demand on my time. And he's worth every minute!

Carmelita, our oldest, is on the other end of the spectrum. As I mentioned, she did great in school because she is a visual learner and schools are geared toward this kind of student. I spend ten to fifteen minutes with her on each subject, and then she goes to her room and finishes her assignment. I could give Carmelita a course syllabus and she would plot out a way to have it completed by the end of the year. If I get too relaxed in my teaching style, however, it makes her nervous. She needs to know that I have a plan, or she will start coming up with one of her own.

The only subject she has struggled with so far is French. So I bought a language software program, and we are learning French together every night after the younger ones go to bed. This has become a special time for us.

Carmelita and I are incredibly different. I'm an outgoing, random-thinking, touchy-feely kind of person, completely opposite of the way she is. I'm afraid that if Carmelita were in school all day, we wouldn't be as close; but because we spend so much time together and relate through school, we have become good friends.

The Eclectic Homeschooler

I love finding the perfect key (like the language software) to unlock each child's understanding. I am a curriculum junkie that way, always on the lookout for the latest and greatest homeschooling tool. My husband sometimes teases me, threatening to ban me from curriculum fairs, cut up my homeschool supply catalogs, and change my password for the used curriculum classifieds sections on my favorite websites.

I'm what you would call an eclectic homeschooler. I don't use one prepackaged curriculum to achieve my goals for each child. I use a little of this, a little of that. I pick a math program that works best for Elena and a different one for Carmelita. I buy some counting bears for Niko, only to resell them a month later when he would rather count his cars. I hear about a fabulous history unit study, and we use that for a while—until I read about an amazing set of historical biographies.

I use all kinds of materials in my teaching. We use educational games and play with toys. We watch videos. We listen to books on tapes. We buy science kits in a box. We draw. We enter contests. Just last month, Elena entered a contest to draw and illustrate her own children's book. (She didn't win, but I did—that was the neatest I've ever seen her print!)

I believe there is value in almost every homeschool resource. That shouldn't be a surprise because most of them are created by homeschooling families who have been using the tools successfully for years in their own homes. We reap the benefit from each tool, then pass it on to another family when we are ready to learn something new, using an entirely different method.

And if I can't find a way to effectively teach a subject, then I find someone who can teach it for me. That's what motivated me to start a homeschool co-op. Actually, I was just looking for someone to give my kids music lessons, but new ideas and new families kept sprouting up until the whole thing mushroomed into a full-fledged co-op. Co-op stands for "cooperative learning," and that simply means we help each other help our children to learn.

We began with just two families. On Friday afternoons I would teach art to my friend Stephanie's kids, and then Stephanie would teach piano to mine. Soon we had recruited a dad who could teach science and another mom who taught drama. Before we knew it, we had eight families with eighteen kids. Then it was eighteen families with thirty-two kids. We finally had to cut it off at twenty families with a total of forty kids.

Since then the co-op has become highly organized. We teach our own children the basics at home in the mornings. Then four days a week we meet at the community center for co-op classes. This semester our schedule has speech and public speaking class being held on Monday afternoons, with a debate planned for the last Monday of each month. Tuesdays, the homeschool band gets together. Wednesday is soccer practice for the homeschool team. Thursday is biology lab. We offer different classes each semester, according to what the parents feel qualified to teach. Every family is required to either teach one class or assist with two. So far we have offered astronomy, Spanish, cooking, woodworking, creative writing, and budgeting, just to name a few.

The beauty is that it's a support group, too. While the other parents are teaching or assisting, the rest of us can sit around and talk and kibitz and laugh. For the children, being a part of a co-op is like having classmates. That in itself is bittersweet, because the day will come when Carlos comes home with more PCS papers and we will have to start all over again. But with homeschooling we have hope. We know we will find friends in the next city—we will simply look up the homeschoolers.

There is a bond between homeschoolers that transcends geographically defined neighborhoods to form an instant community. They will lead me to the best dry

cleaner and dentist, and I will probably have just the curriculum they've wanted to try. I will have friends to hang
out with when Carlos is at sea, and they will take my kids to
the movies when he comes home. They will mention that
they love to sing and I will say, "Hey, have you ever
thought of starting a homeschool co-op? You could teach
choir."

1. Mary Beth Nelsen, quoted by Luz Shosie in Linda Dobson, *The Homeschooling Book of Answers*, revised edition (Roseville, CA: Prima Publishing, 2002), 86.

Chapter Seven

Single Mom, Two Hats

Hello! Perfect timing. I just got the little ones down for a nap. If you don't mind winding your way through the LEGO obstacle course into the kitchen, go ahead and I'll be right there. I need to help my daughter with a quick math problem and then I'll join you. Help yourself to something to drink. I believe you have your choice of milk or a juice box.

THE DARK SIDE OF SOCIALIZATION

Ugh! Geometry! I hated it when I was in school, and I hate it even more now that I'm out of school. Thanks for waiting. Lisa tells me you are thinking about homeschooling. That's awesome! Your children are very lucky—I hope they know that. I wish I had known about homeschooling when *my* kids were little.

Did Lisa tell you anything about my story, or rather my kids' story? Oh, it was heartbreaking. I had no clue what was going on in junior high these days. You see, back in school, I was always one of the popular ones, so I just assumed my children were living the same experience. Boy, was I wrong.

When my husband left us three years ago, our lives were thrown into turmoil and we all responded differently. I needed to support two children, so I found myself hurled into the workforce again with little more to offer than desperation and a high school diploma.

Jamison, who was in sixth grade at the time, turned inward—my happy, outgoing, wisecracking little boy became a sullen, irritable loner.

My eleven-year-old daughter, Staci, seemed to get sweeter every day. She had always been something of a "pleaser," but she became more compliant than ever. I noticed that she was putting on some weight, but I chalked it up to puberty. I still saw her as my beautiful baby girl.

Soon our lives began to settle once again into a routine. It was the three of us against the world—how true that turned out to be.

But Jamie was becoming increasingly moody and withdrew further into his shell. Even I couldn't penetrate it, and we had always been close. I made an appointment to meet with Jamie's history teacher because I had heard Jamie refer to her a couple of times using real words instead of a grunt or a snarl. The moment I met her, I understood why Mrs. Wagner received something other than the usual poison dripping from my son's lips. She was adorable, and she obviously cared about Jamie. Every child should be so lucky as to have a teacher like Mrs. Wagner.

Nothing could have prepared me for what I heard that afternoon. I assumed that Jamie was as hard to get along with at school as he was at home, and I had braced myself to hear about my son the troublemaker. Instead, my knees buckled and my stomach sank as I listened to a painful story of a boy's rejection. My son had spent the last year being ridiculed at school because he wasn't cool enough to fit in.

Why didn't he open up to me? Why couldn't I see beyond the anger to his hurt? Why didn't the school call me? Mrs. Wagner had tried her best to help Jamie, but that only made him more of a target. She explained that her hands were tied because nothing the bullies had done warranted expulsion. The school board's answer to this kind of thing was "That's just life in junior high."

The more he was singled out for torment, the more Jamie was determined not to care. He had fought back by refusing to dress in the most popular fashions or wear his hair in the latest style. Of course, this only made the problem worse.

I didn't know what to do with this new information. In a way, it would have been easier to hear that he was being tied up in the schoolyard and beaten. At least then I could have let loose with my Mama Bear instincts.

Obviously, Jamie didn't want to talk to me about it. His father was physically present every other weekend but never around emotionally. So I sent Jamie to a psychiatrist who prescribed medication, and that helped a little.

On the outside, things gradually appeared to get better for Jamie, but I knew the wound was festering on the inside. I watched news reports of school shootings and, like my friends, worried about the safety of my children. The only difference was, I wondered if it would be *my* son who would someday decide he had taken all he could and choose to take the lives of those who had been snuffing his out little by little.

There had to be more I could do than just stand by helplessly and watch. But what?

I realized I *had* to do something that day in May when my daughter came home sobbing. Through her tears, she told me about the harassment *she* had been enduring every afternoon on the school bus. Because she had begun to develop physically earlier than many of her friends, she had become an object of obsession for a few hormone-filled, movie-fueled, cop-a-feel teenage boys.

Ninth-grade boys were sitting on her lap, touching her, and making suggestive innuendos about things she didn't even understand. The bus driver saw what was going on but didn't do anything to stop it!

That was it. I had to find a way to rescue my children.

LOOKING AT OUR OPTIONS

The next day I marched up to the school with a letter in hand and unenrolled both of my children. Now what was I going to do? I started by doing nothing and allowing Jamie and Staci to do the same. They had both been through so much; they needed time to decompress. I took some vacation time and began looking at our options.

First, I met with the wonderful staff of a local Christian school. They were eager to do all they could to help restore my children's battered souls. I was encouraged just by talking with them. They took me on a tour of their new and impressive facilities. I was met along the way by many fresh, wholesome faces among the students; but I couldn't ignore the dark looks in a smattering of eyes on the periphery.

I came to realize that just because this was a Christian school, that didn't mean all the kids were Christian or even that they had a clear understanding of what *Christian* means. Although the majority of the students were delightful, it was apparent that a few of the students had been sent to the Christian school by parents who thought of it as a pseudo—reform school, hoping their children would "get religion" and get straightened out before the parents had to resort to military school. I was concerned that Jamie was too much of a loner at this time in his life to risk his being the solitary lamb picked off by a big bad wolf in sheep's clothing.

LOTS TO BE LEARNED FROM LIVING

Over the next few weeks, the kids and I came up with a plan we all felt good about. I would concentrate on transitioning from my current job to starting a home day care business in the fall. We determined that it was best for Jamie and Staci to keep doing what they were doing— which was nothing because, hey, nothing was working! They spent the remaining month of the school year reading, playing games together, and much to my delight, becoming pretty good cooks. We found there's lots to be learned from just living!

Slowly, but surely, I got my old kids back. I never would have believed the day would come when I would actually be happy to hear Jamie make another wisecrack about his little sister playing with dolls.

The home day care was a stroke of genius. The little ones are a joy, and the work has allowed me to be here for Jamie and Staci as they continue their education at home.

Video Schooling: A New Hope

That was two years ago and, as you can tell by looking around, our house is full—full of kids, full of love, full of hope, and just plain full. My day begins before the sun rises, because the first toddler arrives shortly after that. Most of the day care children have already been dropped off before my own children fall out of bed and get dressed. After completing their morning chores, Jamie and Staci help me feed the younger ones and get them situated in various baby swings, playpens, video stations, and toy cubbies.

I take advantage of the brief moment of peace that follows and help Jamie and Staci get set up in front of the televisions in their rooms. That's right. You heard me. I actually encourage my kids to plop down in front of the boob tube. That's because we discovered a homeschool curriculum that uses videos. What a lifesaver!

While I take care of the little ones in the other room, my kids learn from a teacher videotaped in front of a classroom. Much of the assigned book work they do on their own, but they often come to me for further explanation. We also take advantage of the day care kids' daily nap time for those lessons that require more concentrated instructional time.

Each day, Jamie watches about two and a half hours of instruction, then completes his assignments on his own.

Staci's classes run about two hours. I check their work against the teacher's manuals, and we discuss any problems they may be having. The teachers on the video are really good, but sometimes I need to explain a concept in a different way before it sinks in with Jamie. Every few weeks, we send the work to the video school company, where they keep track of their grades. They will even issue a high school diploma when all the requirements are met!

After school I care for the babies, play with the toddlers, and teach the preschoolers, while Staci heads to the local equestrian center where she takes riding lessons and helps care for the horses. Three days a week Jamie takes karate at a nearby school, and on the other days he teaches there. His best friend also studies there, and they enjoy hanging out after class. I'm thankful Jamie has the free time to pursue his passion. Making a new friend and discovering something he excels in has made all the difference in the world with his outlook on life.

I wish you could have known Jamie two years ago, because you wouldn't recognize him as the same young man today. He's no longer on medication. Time and, more importantly, learning to forgive brought healing. Jamie is learning how to accept his uniqueness and appreciate the differences in others. His capacity for compassion is a silver lining to an otherwise storm-filled cloud.

So has it all been worth it? Sure, I fall into bed exhausted every night, wondering how long I can keep up this pace. I honestly don't know which will come first, high school graduation or day care burnout. For now, it is enough for me to know that my children are growing into sensitive, self-confident, independent young people—and

I have homeschooling to thank for that.

That's why whenever an uninformed but well-intentioned stranger asks me the favorite homeschool question, "What about the poor child's socialization?" I remind them very gently that they are making the assumption that all socialization is a good thing. In our family's case, it could have been fatal.

Chapter Eight

I Was a Teenage Homeschooler

D id you pass my mom in the driveway? You must have just missed her. My sister called from school. She left some "life or death" cheerleading thing at home, and my mom had to rush it over to her before the big pep rally. It must be hard for Chrissy to bear, knowing the weight of the whole game rests on whether she has her pom-poms or not.

I know you came over to talk to my mom, but I'll be happy to answer any questions you might have. After all, I *am* the guy being homeschooled—and all the way through high school, no less.

So what do you want to know? Let's see. I'm fifteen years old, and I'll be graduating in June. I scored 1450 on my SATs, but I'm not headed for college. I've never attended public school, while my younger sister has never been homeschooled. I don't date but I have lots of "girlfriends." You want me to go on?

Actually, I love messing with people's preconceived ideas about homeschooled teenagers. I'm constantly asked, "Do you feel like you've missed out on anything by not attending high school?" Sure! A one-size-fits-all education, easy access to recreational drugs, my peers worshiping at the altar of *Cool*, dating as a competitive sport, losing my virginity on prom night, and people who judge my worth according to their oblique standards—just to name a few.

I hate to admit it, but some people might consider me a normal high school kid. I've played center in our parks-and-rec basketball league since I was seven. I have two buddies—we grew up together, although few would say we've matured if they've seen us three stooges "nyuking" it up and poking at each other's eyes. It's a guy thing.

I guess the whole "normal" sham breaks down when I admit that I love hanging out with my parents and enjoy talking with my sister into the wee hours of the morning. It gets worse. I thrive on learning and have a clear sense of direction for my life and a plan to get there. The truth is out—I really am abnormal and homeschooling is to blame. I believe the politically correct naysayers were right all along when they said, "Rob your teenager of the high school experience and he may not reach the pinnacle of life at eighteen." Yeah, he may actually continue to grow beyond his yearbook prognostications!

DIFF'RENT STROKES:
ONE AT HOME, ONE AT SCHOOL

I better be careful in case my mom walks through the door and hears me talking like this. You see, she's much less cynical than I am. She believes there is good to be found in almost any situation; it simply depends on how you respond to your circumstances. It's this line of reasoning that keeps my thirteen-year-old sister in public school—as long as she continues to make good choices.

Chrissy is the original social butterfly. She loves the whole idea of lockers, cafeteria food, report cards, and clubs—she's the president of at least a half-dozen of them. Miraculously, she is still at the top of her class academically. To my sister's credit, Chrissy is a natural born leader and takes over every room she enters. That's probably why she's successfully navigating the jungles of junior high— everyone knows where she stands and no one messes with her convictions.

My mom didn't feel like she had what it takes to homeschool such a strong free spirit, so she enrolled Chrissy in public school after an aborted attempt at kindergarten in the kitchen. So far, so good. But don't think I'm not keeping my eye on her. I know my mom is, too. That reminds me, where is my mom? I want you to meet her. She's pretty awesome. Not because she's some Wonder Woman, but because she doesn't try to be.

I admire her for knowing her limitations and being able to make adjustments when she runs into roadblocks. Putting my sister in public school is just one example. And although my mom only has a GED, I'm proud of her for not letting her lack of formal education keep her from homeschooling me.

I'll tell you this much: She was smart enough to know that identifying the parent's teaching style is just as impor-tant as, if not more important than, knowing how your child learns best. I was a "gifted child," and Mom was con-cerned that I would be bored in school, unable to learn at my own pace. So when we first started homeschooling, the "experts" sold my mom on how unit studies would be the best approach for me because I loved to saturate myself in whatever subject fascinated me at the time.

What a calamity! A big piece of information was left out of the sale, and there was a negligent failure to disclose the fact that the unit study approach is a ton of work for a mom and requires a lot of organization. They were right insofar as I did love it! But my mom realized early on that this open-ended approach just didn't work with her personality. You gotta understand, she has a plaque hanging in our kitchen that reads, "Organized people are just too lazy to look for things."

Just over a month into our first unit study on oceans, my mother abandoned the whole experiment and ordered an entire curriculum of first grade workbooks in a box. I'm thankful she didn't throw the baby out with the salt water and pack me off to public school. Once we found a homeschooling method that worked for both of us, it was smooth sailing.

Once we found a homeschooling method that worked for both of us, it was smooth sailing.

My mom settled on the self-instructional curriculum approach because all she had to do was hand me my packets for each subject and rest knowing that the scope-and-sequence requirements were covered. When I was younger, she did a lot more supervising and explaining. As I got older, she simply hovered close by to answer any questions I might have. Everything was so well explained and broken down into bite-size pieces of information that, all in all, I was free to complete the work as quickly as I could—an average of two days of lesson plans each day. Before we realized there was an official name for it, I was well on my way to completing an "accelerated education" program.

That's how I finished twelfth grade by the time I was fourteen. I've spent the last two years taking college-level courses, establishing my own lawn care business, and volunteering at the local nursery (no, not the baby kind). I even had the opportunity to spend six weeks in Mexico with a group of homeschoolers in a Spanish-language immersion program.

Apprenticeship: The Lawn Less Traveled

I've been counting down the days until my sixteenth birthday when my mom will let me officially graduate. Not because I'm particularly thrilled about prancing across a stage in a gown and "mortified board" to receive a rolled-up piece of paper from our homeschool support group. It's because I can't wait to begin my apprenticeship at this amazing landscaping design and maintenance firm across town.

I've been mowing lawns, digging around in gardens, and designing rock creations since I was old enough to peek over the push mower. I am rejuvenated by nature and invigorated by artistic design, and there's just enough modern technology involved in becoming a horticulture technician to keep it intellectually stimulating. Call me crazy, but there's something about the smell of freshly cut grass that is intoxicating to me. Always has been.

And I've been called crazy plenty in my life, but never more vehemently than over my decision not to pursue higher education through college. I don't get it. What's so culpable about wanting to do what I love and love what I do? Sure, God gave me a big brain, but just because I'm not using it to become a doctor or lawyer doesn't mean I'm wasting it. He also gave me an appreciation for beauty and an eye for creating it. Is it less heinous to squander that gift?

Believe me, this is not a decision I arrived at lightly, without examining it from every possible angle. For example, let's look at it from an entirely financial perspective. Even with scholarships, the economic value of an apprenticeship versus going to college is incontrovertible. For example, I will spend the next few years not only working under a mentor who will allow me to benefit from real-life learning in all areas of horticulture, but I will learn to run a small business, as well. That kind of dual major in college would be costly, both in time and money.

And we haven't even begun to discuss the theory of supply and demand. If every parent is grooming his or her child for higher education in order to produce white-collar workers, who is going to be around to fix the plumbing, wire the houses, and put in the lawn sprinklers? And how much will Dr. HMO be willing to pay the few who are truly proficient at these trades?

In going to college you learn a lot of book knowledge about many subjects, and yet graduates often have developed very few practical skills in any one area. The beauty of an apprenticeship is that not only am I receiving this fabulous education in the precise area where I plan to build my future, but I'm also earning a full-time salary. At the completion of my apprenticeship, I will have the expertise and experience I need to go into business for myself. I will be able to do this without going into debt because I will have spent the last few years saving money while your average college student is taking out a small fortune in student loans. That adds up to a pretty good jump start on life.

I think I just heard my mom's car pull into the driveway. One more thing before she walks in. Whether or not you choose to homeschool your kids, remember this: Teenagers still need and, yes, *want* mom around. Sure, two incomes in the home can be nice. But the years and opportunities my mom has sacrificed to stay home with me are the reason I can look forward to my future with expectations and self-confidence. I know I talk a big game, but it's only because I know that, for the next couple of years at least, win or lose, I can always come home to Mom. If I can't persuade you to homeschool, then I'll try to convince you that "home's cool"!

Chapter Nine

Little School in the Big City

Did you have trouble finding a parking spot on the street? I hope you had enough change for the meter; "Lovely Rita" is very punctual when it comes to decorating your windshield with a ticket. Oh, the joys of living downtown. I'm only being slightly facetious. As long as I keep my mind on the benefits of city life, then I don't miss suburbia so much. And there are many tremendous advantages to living in a big city, especially for a homeschooler on a budget.

You can't beat the opportunities for creative excursions—and I'm the Queen of Field Trips. I'm not talking about your run-of-the-mill trip to the zoo, either. We can walk into almost any business, restaurant, or retail outlet any day of the week and learn something new. You might be surprised how willing people are to take the time to teach a child about what they do for a living. I think it reminds them that what they are doing is valuable and interesting.

Here in the city we have the world at our doorstep—well,

down the hall, out the elevator, through the lobby, and out the revolving door, anyway. And I do mean the world, not simply America. The city offers not only a multitude of cultural experiences, but a host of *multicultural* experiences as well. We haven't had any trouble providing our children with a broader worldview than knowing that pizza comes from Italy, croissants from France, and rice from China.

Of course, it's hard to find a better classroom than a museum. Because we live so close to everything, we are able to stroll through an art museum on our lunch break, spend an afternoon at an interactive science center, or take in a traveling dinosaur exhibit at the natural history museum. The downtown public library is practically our home away from home. Every once in a while, it helps to count these blessings. I'm glad you came over today—I needed the boost.

We moved here when my husband was laid off from his job in the suburbs. For months we struggled to keep our house and white-picket-fence lifestyle. By the time he was offered this job downtown, we were grateful for any job that would help us put food on the table. Of course, I could have gone back to work; but I've been there and done that, and I'd rather give up just about anything than the privilege of raising our children myself.

I have a degree in early childhood development, and before we had children of our own, I worked as a preschool teacher. I saw the same children from seven o'clock in the morning until six o'clock at night, and I wondered why their parents even bothered having children at all. I was the one who got to witness their first steps, hear their first complete sentences, and wipe their noses and their tears. I wasn't willing to give some stranger twice as much time as I got in the day to shape and mold my child. I wanted to be the one who was rocking the cradle and ruling my child's world.

We counted the cost and decided our children were worth it. So our only hope of survival was to downsize dramatically. We sold our house in the 'burbs and rented this apartment in the city. With public transportation so accessible, we pared down to one car. Eating out is a rare treat, but to be honest, I like this scenario better than the other all-too-common extreme where a home-cooked meal around the family table is a rare treat. We are grateful for the many hand-me-downs we receive from family, friends, and other homeschoolers. We can't afford the latest fashions for the kids, so homeschooling has been a plus in that sense, because fashion is not so much of an issue on a daily basis.

Curriculum on a Budget

We kind of backed into homeschooling. Private school was obviously out of the question for us financially, and I had heard too many horror stories about the city school. So we looked into homeschooling. At first it was our only choice; now it is a conviction and I wouldn't give it up if we had all the money in the world.

Not that we haven't had to come up with some creative curriculum choices to supplement our "big city" education. My husband's annual income is under forty thousand dollars a year, so there isn't a lot left over for homeschool supplies. Thankfully, that really isn't necessary. Entire books have been written on how to homeschool your children for free, and they aren't exaggerating.

I learned the very first year to avoid the curriculum fairs; they are simply too tempting. I want everything they are selling, and it's hard to remind myself that I really don't need all the latest educational toys, supplies, and curriculum packages to provide my children with a complete education. I do make an exception for used curriculum sales. But even then I try to hold myself back and not show up until the end of the day. More than once I have discovered that many of the booth operators would rather *give* you what they have left over than have to pack it up and cart it back home. It's like Christmas in July when we get home and dig through the newly acquired boxes of treasure. What's funny is that I usually end up giving most of it away myself six months later to other homeschoolers.

Occasionally I decide I just have to buy the latest math manipulatives, educational software, historical video, or craft kit. So the first place I check is the Internet homeschool classifieds sites and the discount bookstores on-line.

Of course, it is hard to beat *free,* and unless you abuse it, television is a wonderful source, especially the public broadcast stations. We can't afford cable, but my sister-in-law is always on the lookout for historical and scientific shows to videotape and send to us. We studied the Civil War by watching an incredible anthology on the subject. Sometimes one thing leads to another and we find ourselves following bunny trails on to related subjects. That happened with these videos.

We became so interested in that period of American history that we read everything we could get our hands on about every aspect, from slavery to Abe Lincoln to muskets. Thank goodness for the Internet. I've always believed that there is no more effective way to teach a child than simply encourage questions and be around to answer them. But sometimes you find yourself stumped. That's when it's nice to be able to seize upon their enthusiasm and search for the answers together—the operative word being *together*. Although we have done all we can to protect our children by installing an Internet filter and teaching them how to navigate the potential land mines, it is still wisest to surf the Web together. Besides, I've learned so much in the process myself. I know for a fact that I've learned more in the years I have been teaching my children than in my entire career as a student. I *love* learning now! And my children do, too, which is infinitely more important to me.

Procuring a computer was also much easier than I anticipated. I am amazed at how many people upgrade their machines once a year. One day at work, my husband offhandedly mentioned that his wife was looking for a good deal on a computer for the children's education, and someone immediately offered him their used system—free! I guess they were as thrilled to get rid of their "dinosaur" as we were to welcome it into our family. One man's dinosaur is another man's kitty cat (and mouse).

> I love learning now! And my children do, too.

While the world is at our doorstep, the World Wide Web is on our desktop. The amount of homeschooling resources on the Internet blow my mind. There are links to teacher support groups, lesson plans, record-keeping utilities, organizational tips, legal answers, tests, scope and sequences, and guides for teaching different age and grade levels.

For the student there are thousands of sites that focus on study skills, reference materials, sentence diagramming, spelling rules, reading comprehension, creative writing, basic math, advanced algebra, art, music appreciation, crafts, government, archeology, biology, paleontology—in fact, all of the -ologies.

As you can see, it is possible to homeschool your child on a budget all the way through high school. I have a daughter from a previous marriage who is attending a nearby university on a full scholarship, and I homeschooled her from ninth grade on. She was able to enroll in a few classes at the local community college during her junior and senior years in high school. This was especially helpful for the labs and advanced math requirements, and she earned high school and college credits at the same time. When she began looking at universities, we were surprised to learn that, despite misconceptions regarding home education, many of the finest schools are now actively recruiting homeschoolers. Why? Because they tend to be self-motivated and more involved in community service and extracurricular activities, and they consistently score higher on standardized achievement tests than their public school counterparts.

The Flexible Family

Academics is just one aspect of the advantages homeschool enjoys over public education. We learned this firsthand four years ago, when my mother was diagnosed with cancer and the flexibility to care for an aging parent was suddenly a tremendous side benefit of homeschooling. For months I walked a fine line between taking care of my parents and not neglecting my husband. Every few weeks I would pack up the children, hop on a bus, and move back into my childhood home. We took advantage of these trips by playing games along the way.

Our favorite was to create math problems for each other. Math really comes alive when you apply it to real life. For example, I'd say, "What if Grandpa gave each of you three nickels. How many cents would you have? Now one of you buys a piece of gum that costs a dime—how much money do you have left over? If you put all of your change together, how many additional pieces of gum could you buy?" Tell me that isn't a lot more fun and challenging than most first grade textbooks. The kids begged for more, and it sure made the trip go faster.

We homeschooled everywhere *except* home that year—on the bus, in hospital waiting rooms, at the doctor's office, and in my parents' backyard. I felt like I was short-changing my children the last six months because I simply bought them each a huge grade-level workbook from Wal-Mart and assigned them worksheets every day. Boy, was I surprised when they took the standardized tests and all of them scored between the eightieth and ninetieth percentile at the end of that year.

Even if that hadn't been the case, many of the lessons they learned during that year could never be measured on a chart. How do you put a grade on the wisdom accumulated by sitting for hours, listening to Grandpa tell stories about his life growing up on a farm in the early 1900s? Or having the home health care nurse explain how the little cuff around Grandma's arm gradually fills with air to press the artery and how, using her stethoscope, the nurse listens to the noise emitted by the blood as it passes through the artery to measure Grandma's blood pressure. And nobody can convince me that laying kitchen tile with Grandpa isn't a wonderful geometry lesson.

The benefits far outweighed the phonics rules that year, but none more than my kids' witnessing the stream of people come through that tiny bedroom door and return a portion of the love that my mother has poured out her whole life. These kinds of lessons in sacrifice, compassion, service, and integrity cannot be taught in a classroom situation.

After my mother passed away, the rest of the family had to rush off to jobs and schools. We were able to stay a few more weeks and support my father through the loss of his beloved bride of forty-six years. The precious gift of time and memories cannot be recovered when your children must log a certain amount of days behind a desk in order to move on in life. After all, life isn't about being there for roll call—it's about *being there*.

Every once in a while, I think about what our life would be like if my husband still had his former job and we still lived in our old neighborhood. My children would more than likely all be in public school. They would be wearing the latest sneakers, and we would be rushing them back and forth between lessons and practices. I would be involved in the PTA, and we would probably have more *stuff.*

But what does it profit a mom if she gains the whole world and loses her children, their hunger for knowledge, their compassion, and their appreciation for things that are of real value (as opposed to what the typical American child considers important). Sometimes less really is more.

Chapter Ten

Free to Be Keaton: My ADHD Child

Come on around—I'm in the backyard. I hope you don't mind if we talk outside. It's such a beautiful day, and I love watching Keaton play in the backyard with his friend Jeffrey. They've built some kind of contraption with a ball of string and a pulley for their army guys. They crack me up. Watching how they play, you would never guess that they're both twelve years old. They act like they're still seven, but I love that about them.

Keaton's buddies Chester and Scott are the same way. They can play for hours with a box or anything with wheels. You should see some of the "movies" they've made with my video camera—they are priceless. Keaton is an only child, so I don't take his friends for granted.

You see, friends have been hard to come by over the years. For one thing, little boys with ADHD (attention deficit hyperactivity disorder), like Keaton, aren't often invited back to other children's houses. Usually, the mothers just can't handle their energy, and the fathers have a difficult time coping with their nonstop talking. It helps to find boys like Scott who also have ADHD, or other only children, like Chester. I usually drive over to pick up Keaton's friends and bring them over to our house, and they sometimes end up staying for days. This works out well for everyone. The other parents enjoy the break, knowing their son is well cared for. And I'm happy because Keaton is happy.

Boys love Keaton. He is full of grand ideas and elaborate plans. He never stops moving. He never stops talking. He never walks; he runs everywhere. He is fearless and daring. He always has a smile on his face, and he knows how to put one on yours. Did I mention he's hysterically funny? Thank the Lord!

Laughing has been the saving grace of our relationship. Ask anyone who is raising an ADHD kid and they will tell you: It is hard. Very hard. I don't know what I would do without the support of my husband, Pete, and Scott's mother, Candace, telling me that I'm okay, I will survive, and sometimes more importantly, Keaton will survive.

I often find myself asking the question, *Isn't consistency supposed to pay off someday?* I feel like I'm always saying the same things again and again, wondering if Keaton will ever "get it." At least I have this to hold on to: Even if he never changes, I have changed enough for the both of us. Being the parent of an ADHD child works wonders in the areas of patience, acceptance, self-control, and flexibility.

Over the years I have picked up quite a few coping techniques—tricks, you might say. For one thing, when he was little and I tried to teach Keaton something relatively simple like tying his shoes, how to address an envelope, or the correct way to fold blue jeans, I learned that I must clear the deck of everything else. I couldn't just expect to show him how to do it then move on to answering my e-mail or slicing vegetables for dinner and trust that he would simply pick it up or keep practicing until he mastered it. I needed to sit beside him in a calm environment, maintaining eye contact and giving him my full attention.

Another key I found is not to throw too many things at him at once. I've learned to break down potentially overwhelming tasks into smaller, manageable chunks. For example, right now his bedroom looks like it was ravaged by a hurricane. If I were to send Keaton upstairs with instructions not to come down until his room was clean, he would still be up there a week from now. Instead I tell him to clean off his dresser, then go outside and shoot fifty hoops. After that I instruct him to make his bed, clean out from under it, and then join me for a glass of milk and a couple of cookies. Now that he's fortified, he can pick up everything off the floor and put it in its place before jumping on the trampoline for fifteen minutes. Finally he can tackle the closet, and then he is all done!

It really helps to provide an outlet for his endless supply of energy. That trampoline was the best investment we ever made. I have found that if he starts the day off by jumping or running or climbing or swinging, then it's easier for him to focus on the day ahead.

But the most important element in Keaton's life is structure. There is so much going on inside his mind and body that he desperately needs the consistency of a schedule. It may not be readily apparent to an observer, but there is

definitely a certain rhyme and reason to our day. Keaton
gets up at the same time every morning and goes to bed early
each night. He has the same daily chores, regular mealtimes,
and rules that don't change.

When Keaton started school, I thought he would do
fine because he has always responded well to routine. What
I soon discovered, however, was that home provided him
freedom within a structure. His classroom was just the
opposite, offering confinement within chaos. I read
somewhere that conventional schools can be failure traps
for children who, by nature, are not quiet, compliant
morning people able to concentrate for long periods of
time. This is especially true for kids who are unable to
screen out a lot of distracting sounds and activities.[1]

So my son was failing first grade! I didn't even know
that was *possible,* especially for someone as bright as Keaton.
We had weekly meetings with his teacher, Miss Fender. She
said he wasn't catching on in either reading or math. We
learned that one of the reasons he was failing was because
he couldn't remember to turn in his class work. He just
put it in his desk, and Miss Fender never thought to look
in his desk for his missing work. She just gave him zeros.

Worse, he was in trouble all the time. His self-esteem
was crushed, as he was labeled a problem child by most of
the faculty. Miss Fender thought that by pointing out the
fact that he already had five demerits by lunchtime, it
would motivate Keaton to try harder to be better. Instead,
it only alienated him from the other kids, whom he was
already having trouble getting along with.

When he came home saying that he was going to go to
prison when he grew up because he was bad, I knew we

had to do something. We took him to the doctor, who diagnosed what we had already guessed, and we came home with a prescription for Ritalin. I kept it in my purse for the longest time, not wanting to get it filled. I was worried because there hadn't been many studies on the long-term effects of Ritalin. When Keaton entered second grade, the same cycle began. Except this time we met for weekly parent-*principal* meetings. We decided that the long-term effects of the medication couldn't be much worse than the effects of ADHD.

At first, Ritalin was like a miracle drug. Keaton was able to concentrate and prove to his teacher—and more importantly, to himself—that he was actually very smart. He not only absorbed concepts more quickly, but he was also able to sit still and not talk for more than five minutes at a time. This made a world of difference in his teacher's eyes, and he began to make friends among the other students. His self-esteem soared.

Unfortunately, there *were* side effects from the medication. Keaton wasn't eating or sleeping well, and the doctor warned us that it was possible his growth could be stunted. And it was a little like living with Dr. Jekyll and Mr. Hyde. Keaton was either coming down off the drug and slamming doors or he was walking around like a zombie. Sometimes I didn't recognize my own little boy. He started begging me to take him off the medication; he said that it made him feel like his real self was trapped inside and couldn't get out.

I decided to try an experiment. One weekend, after taking Keaton off the meds for a few days, I read a book to him and required him to sit still and pay attention.

Afterwards I asked him to tell me the basic story, but he couldn't remember so much as a quarter of it. The next day I let him tumble on the floor, play LEGOs, draw, and color while I read another book to him. Later I asked him to retell the story to me, and he could recite it almost verbatim! Perhaps he did learn more when he was constantly moving.

A few days later, I was helping him with his math homework. He was hanging upside down in the kitchen chair with his feet up in the air and his math page on the table. I was getting frustrated with him, so I grabbed the paper and began calling out the problems to him. To my amazement, he began shouting out the answers instantly. He was adding numbers like thirty-six and seven in his head. Double-digit, carry-the-one, mental math! This was the kid who got a D on his last math test.

I had grown tired of the school focusing on his disabilities rather than his abilities. Keaton was obviously a bright, sweet kid; he just didn't fit into a standard classroom situation. It was actually my husband who came up with the idea for us to homeschool. I don't know what I thought homeschooling was like, but I was not prepared for what it turned out to be.

From the start it was easier than I expected. Keaton's behavior was nothing like it was in school where he reacted to all of the classroom stimuli. Homeschooling removed these behavioral triggers, not to mention the stress, the peer pressure, and the canned instructions given to thirty students at once. We quickly realized that homeschooling was going to be a lifesaver for Keaton.

Still, I was nervous about how I was going to be able to

handle my ADHD child all day long, much less teach him. I decided the only way I could do it was to take a relaxed approach. After researching all the different methods, we discovered that there was actually a name for what we had been doing since Keaton was a baby—providing freedom within structure. It was called *unschooling*.

UNSCHOOLING

It is very difficult to define unschooling, but I'll try. The unschooling approach is based on the conviction that our children are born with an innate desire to learn, and that they will learn if we simply trust them to pursue their interests on *their* timetable. Not that I don't lead my son to water. We don't allow any television or video or computer games. Instead, he fills his time and brain with other fun things—like learning!

When I tell people about unschooling, I often hear, "But don't kids need to learn that there are things they just *have* to do? We can't go through life doing only what we *feel* like doing." These people are always surprised when I agree with them. Of course there are things my son has to do, like brushing his teeth, going to bed at a decent hour, doing his chores, going on family outings, and using good manners. And I expect Keaton to obey me when I ask him to do something, even though he certainly doesn't always feel like doing what is asked of him.

The skeptics can't comprehend that kids learn math on their own because they *want* to. Keaton studies grammar, history, and science—and he learns all these subjects in depth. Maybe because the skeptics learned to do things how and when they were told, they just can't comprehend that a child will actually enjoy learning something that, in their day, was dull and dry. This is evidence of how very well "schooled" we adults are.

Many home educators, when they first hear about unschooling, will have an immediate negative response to it. These parents probably shouldn't unschool, and of course, they don't have to because there are so many other methods. On the other hand, there will be some who look back on their traditional education and think, *Ninety percent of what I'm now using in my life and career is stuff that I learned on my own, either outside of school or after I graduated.* For them, unschooling will seem a much more viable option.

I find it ironic that we all were unschooled to some degree, both before compulsory school and after graduation, but we leave it up to professionals to tell us what our own children should learn in between. We've all basically unschooled our children from birth and just didn't realize it. I've always tried to provide Keaton with educational toys, picture books, puzzles, paper, crayons, and even alphabet place mats. But mostly we provided him with plenty of time to play, which is the work of childhood.

One thing we have consistently done from the beginning is read to Keaton. You can imagine how shocked I was to discover that he couldn't even read three-letter words when we pulled him out of school in the second grade. Thankfully, I had read a book encouraging parents not to push their kids to grasp concepts before they were ready. I like this philosophy. Why do schools teach and reteach the same things over and over again every year throughout the elementary grades? Doesn't it make more sense to wait until the child is ready and then teach it to him once? Think about how absurd it would be to work every day with a five-month-old baby, trying to teach him how to walk. Until his brain and muscles were more fully developed, it just wouldn't happen. Sure, he may walk a week or two early as a result of my efforts, but what is the point of that? He would eventually learn to walk on his own.

So until Keaton was ready to read on his own, I simply took advantage of the precious time to read to him. I miss those days of his sitting on my lap while I followed the words with my finger and he "read" the books with me. Nowadays I have to fight the tendency to be jealous of his books. He loves nothing better than to lay outside on the trampoline by himself, reading a good story.

Children who love to read are usually very easy to unschool because their own passion for learning is often enough to motivate them. Most learning can be accomplished by reading good books. I border on the compulsive when it comes to stocking our family library. We have shelves and shelves of every imaginable kind of book: science, historical fiction, cartoons, biographies, how-to books—anything and everything I can find at garage sales or the library's used-book sales.

Children who love to read are usually very easy to unschool.

Keaton is a whiz at science and history, and I haven't specifically taught him a lot on either subject. What he knows he has learned mostly by reading biographies. I discovered early on the power of a time line for history and a globe for geography. These have given him tangible places to "hang" new information he discovers in books. I'll never forget the day he burst into the kitchen with the news flash that the first submarine was invented before men began shaving.

But what do you do if your child doesn't enjoy reading? Don't worry about it. Listen to a classic book on tape in the car. Play a story tape at bedtime. Watch the History Channel or A&E's *Biography*. There are plenty of fun and interesting ways to learn besides reading. Don't get me started on real life as education or we'll be here all afternoon.

I find it hysterical when I hear people speculate that Keaton won't be prepared to deal with the real world when he grows up because he has been sheltered at home. I want to say, "Wait a minute, which child is shut up in a classroom all day long and which one is at the grocery store, at the bank, and in the garden?" It's hard to convince someone that what looks like "doing nothing" all day is actually more valuable in an adult's life than most of what is learned in textbooks. That's one of the reasons why I think report cards and grades are ridiculous. How do you determine a grade when your child keeps trying new things until he finally discovers something that stops his baby niece from crying? Where on a report card do I quantify learning how to read a map on the way to Grandma's house? Hey, I know what Keaton does and doesn't know; I don't need to measure it against the so-called average student.

Not that I'm against keeping track of Keaton's

progress. I simply call it scrapbooking. That sounds so much more fun and, really, I'm doing it for my future daughter-in-law, not because someone is telling me that I have to. Keaton loves to look through his scrapbook at how much more legible his cursive writing is now than when he was in third grade. He giggles when he looks at early "masterpieces" of art complete with his four-year-old's signature.

I am a photography fanatic, so I have included pictures of Keaton with just about every creation he has ever built—science experiments, Play-Doh sculptures, field trip crafts. My favorite pages are those filled with things he has written. I keep thank-you notes, poems, letters to Aunt Phyllis, love notes to Mommy, and "school stuff," like the time I asked him to write down why he thought Einstein was the smartest man who ever lived. Keaton wrote about the fact that Einstein kept in his closet several suits of exactly the same style and color, so that he never had to waste mental energy on something as mundane as choosing what he would wear for the day.

One of Keaton's favorite facts about Einstein is that he never memorized anything he could look up, including his own phone number. I tend to agree with Einstein's approach, especially when it comes to rote facts. I would much prefer that Keaton know how to find information that he can use rather than commit to memory a bunch of dates and statistics that he will never need. Usefulness should be a *major* criteria for learning. History is useful, not because we *should* know the names of famous people, but because learning from our past will help keep us from making the same mistakes. Science is useful, not because we might be on *Jeopardy!* someday, but because understanding the foundations of life allows us to explore creation more deeply.

Surprisingly, math is one of the easiest subjects to unschool, mainly because it is so doggone useful. The first time Keaton earned an allowance and was turned loose in a toy store, he understood the importance of math: *How much money will I have left if I buy this LEGO kit that's on sale for 20 percent off?* Keaton has learned math through cooking, playing with dominoes, using calculators, estimating, doing word problems, and even maneuvering magnetic letters. When he was only seven years old, Keaton was messing around with the alphabet on the fridge when he made a square with five letters on each side. He thought out loud, "I wonder what five times five equals?" After counting them up and discovering the answer was twenty-five, he lined more up and said, "Now let's see what six times six equals." Remember, this was going on at the same time he was failing math at school.

How and why then was he able to learn multiplication? Because he was interested in it at that time and because he enjoyed discovering the answers to his questions. That's why one of my favorite terms for unschooling is *interest-led learning.* There are other names for the same thing: *delight-driven, child-initiated, natural learning, experienced-based learning,* and *independent learning.*

Engaging a child's interest is so important because children retain much more when they are interested and self-motivated. When Keaton gets wrapped up in something, he pursues it like a boy obsessed. Contrast that with his teachers who complained that he was so easily distracted that he couldn't learn anything without being drugged. What is the difference? Interest.

When Keaton was little he was interested in bugs, so he collected them, identified them, read about them, and labeled them, until his interest shifted to the military. At that point, he began watching old war movies, played with G. I. Joes, idolized the Navy SEALS, exercised using military calisthenics, and memorized all the different military ranks. That is, until he became interested in trains. And then cartooning. And then making money. Currently, he is saturating himself with information about cars.

These may all be valuable pursuits, but they are not what I set my eyes and heart to look out for from the time he was born. I am watching and waiting for that one thing that sets Keaton on fire with a passion that isn't snuffed out by the next passing fancy. It may be a few more years before that flame ignites, but when it does, then I will feel like my job is done. Because once Keaton discovers what he was born to do, nothing will be able to stop him.

That is the goal of homeschooling for me. I want to prepare Keaton for life—and not just anybody's life, but his own unique destiny.

---

1. Susan Evans, quoted by Linda Dobson, *The Homeschooling Book of Answers*, revised edition (Roseville, CA: Prima Publishing, 2002), 44.

Chapter Eleven

Full Quiver, Full House

D o you mind if we sit out here on the front porch? It's such a pretty day, and I can keep an eye on the little ones playing by the chicken coop. Molly, would you get our friends a glass of lemonade? Emily, I need you to check on the baby and make sure she is still asleep. James, did you finish folding the laundry? Come here, Sarah, climb up in Mommy's lap and lay your head down—you look like you're coming down with something.

Okay, I think I have all my little ducks in a row. We should have at least five minutes' peace to talk. Never a dull moment when you have ten children. Oh don't worry, drink your lemonade. We had the water tested and discovered that wasn't what was causing it.

The second question we are always asked is "Were they all planned?" (The first is usually "Are you Mormon or Catholic?") The answer is, yes, they were planned—just not by us.

You see, we don't think God was crazy when He said that

children are a reward. The Bible says that children are like arrows in the hand of a warrior. "Happy, blessed, and fortunate is the man whose quiver is filled with them!" (Psalm 127:5). I would be the crazy one if I responded to God's blessings with, "Please don't give me any more rewards!"

I understand that not everyone feels this way and that's fine. We just know that raising a large family is our calling. If we are supposed to be making a difference in the world, what better way to do it than by training our children to become beacons to the world?

Many parents who choose to homeschool do so because they want to be the primary influence in their kids' lives. Indeed, our responsibility—I like to think of it as our *privilege*—to train our children and shape their character is the main reason we homeschool. You can't schedule a "teachable moment," and the less time you spend with your children, the fewer opportunities you will have to seize these moments when they present themselves.

We believe that discipline is foundational—not only for a positive homeschool experience but also for a successful life experience—and I don't want to leave it up to someone else to make sure my children develop good character traits in addition to good study habits. I'm not just referring to correcting the children when they make poor choices; we also try to catch them making good choices and point out when they demonstrate obedience, selflessness, diligence, initiative, honesty, and the like.

Did I forget to mention the benefit of good, old-fashioned hard work to develop character? Living on a small farm provides us with plenty of fruit, vegetables, eggs, poultry, milk, sunshine, and unlimited opportunities for responsibility. The children are learning life skills early and thus confidence. Because everyone needs to pitch in and help, they feel like they're a part of something bigger. It's certainly less of a struggle to instill selflessness when everything revolves around what is best for the family as a whole, instead of the individual.

There are plenty of jobs to go around. We have two dogs, two cats, and a bunny for the younger ones to care for. The horses, chickens, laying hens, turkeys, and goats are fed, watered, and cleaned by the boys. The girls oversee the garden, which includes planting, harvesting, canning, pickling, freezing, putting beans up, drying the herbs, and picking and pressing the berries. Do you see the opportunities for homeschooling in the midst of chores? Last week, Isaac learned the biology of a turkey when he shot it, plucked it, and cleaned it. Tell me that isn't more fun than a science textbook!

We incorporate much of our rural life into the family's 4-H projects and call it schoolwork. One of the highlights of the year is the state fair, when we get to demonstrate many of the things we've been working on all year long. 4-H isn't just about animals anymore. At one time or another, our children have tried their hands at public speaking, dance, photography, entomology, record keeping, quilting, bread baking, forestry, rocketry, woodworking, electricity, and of course, horticulture, and livestock.

The Simple Life

As you can probably imagine, running a farm (albeit small), raising a family (unquestionably large), and homeschooling (undeniably time-consuming) takes major organizational planning and scheduling. How do we do everything? Well, we *don't* do a lot of things. People complain, but I don't answer the phone during the day; I let the machine pick it up. It's just too easy to get sidetracked.

We don't own a television, and although we have a computer, I rarely have time to answer e-mail. We really only use the computer to do research on occasion. We must make every moment count. Even time in the car, running errands, is used to take turns reading aloud. Not the driver, of course. I'm talking on the cell phone. Just kidding!

Every minute of the day is basically planned ahead. We have a master calendar posted on the kitchen bulletin board so that everyone knows what they need to be doing at any given time. My husband, Grant, and I usually rise before dawn to have our morning devotions and quiet time to talk with each other over a cup of coffee. This is so important to our marriage (and my sanity).

While I shower and get dressed, Grant wakes up the older kids, oversees breakfast, and reads the Bible and a book to them while they are eating. Once I'm finished with my morning routine, I get the baby and the two-year-old up and dressed, while Grant gets ready and heads off to work. By this time the "cleaning crew" is ready to go, and I get them started on their chores.

The children rotate job responsibilities, taking turns doing laundry, washing dishes, sweeping, mopping, vacuuming, scrubbing toilets, dusting, and general housekeeping. I already mentioned the farm duties; they get taken care of at this time, too. In the meantime, I take care of the little ones, getting them fed and changed and teaching them. Homeschooling at this age is limited mainly to picture books, foam puzzles, stacking toys, and lots of cuddling. While they watch from the high chair and Sassy Seat, I lay out and prepare the items for dinner that night.

Once the chores are all done, it is time to begin "real" school. I primarily use unit studies to homeschool, but we still do math and phonics separately. We don't have a set place for this, like a schoolroom. As often as not, you can find the kids doing their work under a table, in the tire swing, in the back of the pickup, or in a pile of hay. While the older ones are doing their math, I work with the beginners on their reading.

We don't often do school past lunch. While the kids clean up after the meal, I put the three youngest down for a nap—and I sometimes put myself down for a nap! The older kids spend time quietly in their rooms reading, resting, and practicing their Scripture verses for Awana, a weekly Bible-based kids' activity program offered locally through our church.

I try to keep the afternoons free for the children to relax and just be kids. This is the time of the day when I run errands, take care of correspondence, do needlepoint, and enjoy a cup of hot tea before making my "appointment" with each child. That may sound sterile, but it is actually very special. Every day I spend an hour devoted to one particular child. We work on problem school areas, talk about heart issues, play cards, or simply hang out together.

Before long the hustle and bustle starts up again, as it is time to prepare for Daddy's arrival and dinnertime.

Everyone pitches in and chops, cleans, stirs, bakes, and sets the table. When Grant gets home, we all gather around the table and make a joyful noise—a very loud joyful noise.

Each evening something different is planned. The kids love Monday night because they get to see all of their friends at church and play games at Awana. Tuesday night is Mom and Dad's date night. Wednesday night is Bible study at the Gardners' house. Thursday night is a quiet evening at home. Friday night is Family Night. Saturday is usually a work day around the farm, so we keep the evening rather low-key. And Sunday is church.

Most of the time we are all in bed by nine or nine-thirty at the latest. We usually turn in early because the next day we do it all over again. I wouldn't be honest if I didn't tell you that some days, when the alarm rings, I'm tempted to pull the covers over my head and call in sick. I've been home-schooling for fifteen years and I "quit" about once every year. But then I stop and remember why we started home-schooling in the first place. Do I really want them learning evolution as fact, politically correct agendas, rewritten history, tolerance as a subject, and how to put on a condom?

We gather around the table and make a joyful noise—a very loud joyful noise.

No, I want my children to marvel at God's creation and seek out answers as to how it all works together. I want them to understand the power of words and be capable of reaching their potential for influence, both written and spoken, for the good of mankind. I want them to appreciate order and understand the mathematical formulas for achieving it. I want them to know where they are going by learning from those who have gone before.

Unit Studies: One Topic, Many Subjects

I have found unit studies to be a wonderful way to teach these things to our family. It's also a practical way to teach a whole houseful of children at different grade levels at the same time. That issue in itself scares some parents away from homeschooling. I find it ironic that we expect a public schoolteacher to teach thirty boys and girls of varying interests, backgrounds, and skill levels, but many of us don't think we can handle our own family.

Let me take you through our most recent six-week unit study on the solar system, which focused on God and intelligent design. Science was easy; we simply studied the planets, stars, and everything else floating around in outer space. For history, we studied the famous astronomers and explorers. Certainly, there is plenty of math involved in calculating the distance from the sun to everything else out there. Language arts consisted of reading aloud *From the Earth to the Moon* by Jules Verne, copying passages from the book for penmanship and grammar, writing reports about each planet, and spelling words like *telescope, constellation,* and *Galileo.*

The beauty of unit studies is your ability to cover all subjects for all ages at all levels. I pick a topic and just expect that some of them are going to get a lot more out of it than others. I am able to gently lead my slower learner and rush ahead with my racehorse child. Everyone has a chance to get in on the fun. Since all the material is integrated—rather than presented in unrelated bits and pieces—children make connections more readily, boosting their retention.

For example, for our final report we put on a "solar system walk" for Dad. The younger children drew, colored, labeled, and cut out each planet and glued it on a coat hanger. The older children each thoroughly researched two planets and the sun. Then they used their math skills to measure the area and calculate the relative distances at which we would need to put the planets.

Then we put on a show. Each child read one of their reports aloud before pulling out the props. Using a lamp for the sun, the globe for the Earth, and a ball for the moon, the children "explained" to Dad (and the little listening ears) everything they had learned about the seasons, year, moon phases, tides, constellations, explorers, eclipses, etc. We were able to see the eclipse shadows and moon phases as the children demonstrated.

It was a beautiful spring evening, so afterward we spread out a blanket, ate dinner on the lawn, and lay out under the stars. If I ever wondered whether unit studies were a great way to teach my children, I will never doubt it again after that night. Grant was attempting to see how much our first grader had understood by pointing out the Big Dipper. Little Joshua came back with, "No, Daddy, that is Ursa Major. Can't you see the Drinking Gourd is the bear's tail?"

That brings me to the next most common question I'm asked: "How do you homeschool with a newborn, a toddler, and a preschooler in the house?" My philosophy is, if you can't beat 'em, ask 'em to join you! It is truly amazing how much they pick up just by being in the room while you teach.

Remember, the older children do their math and grammar work earlier in the morning while I spend one-on-one time loving the wee ones. This seems to create a measure of contentment so they don't feel like they are always competing for my attention.

Before we begin our unit study, I put the baby down for her morning nap. If Jeremiah, our two-year-old, is being fussy, then he is ushered into his room with a bunch of safe toys and a baby gate across the door. Otherwise, he joins preschooler Gracie in the kitchen where we're having school. They have a special tote bag of "school supplies" like baby scissors, crayons, books, and counting bears. Once the thrill of the bag wears off, we pull out a box of toys that are saved for school time only. I rotate the toys in this box often to keep them exciting and "new." Many of my friends keep sing-a-long videos for kids of this age on their crankier days.

By far the most effective and rewarding way I have found to homeschool with tiny ones is to ask the older ones to teach them. Oftentimes I will say, "Isaac, honey, please go read to your baby sister until I finish helping James," or "Elizabeth, will you help Gracie trace her letters?" My oldest children truly enjoy teaching their younger siblings. I can't count the number of times I have listened quietly while one of them explained to a younger child why the ocean is salty, how cold it is on Pluto, or how dust mixes inside a flower to make a piece of fruit.

That's another reason I like unit studies so much—the

connectedness, each element pointing back to a theme. Just like family relationships—each individual working together to build a whole. In the beginning, I was tempted to jump through all of the traditional academic hoops until I stopped and asked myself, *What do I really want for my daughters and sons when they grow up and leave this house?* I want my sons to become stalwart leaders with strong servant's hearts. I want to train them to be good husbands by requiring them to treat their sisters with respect and care. Grant is making sure they have the mind-set and practical skills to be the providers, protectors, and spiritual heads of their homes.

I want to model respect for my husband in front of all my children, but especially for my daughters. I want to prepare them for higher education, should they choose to pursue a degree. At the same time I want to show them by example that being a stay-at-home mom is perhaps the most rewarding vocation in the world.

I guess a lot depends on how you measure success. My children still believe I'm the best mother in the world, that their father is wise, and that it is cool to live in the same house with their best friends. Homeschooling does not create perfect children who never compete with one another or squabble, but it can create close ties between family members who naturally come to know each other better because of the time they spend together. That is what I call success. Family identity—relationships—connectedness. A unity study.

Chapter Twelve

To Grandmother's House We Go

D o you like gingerbread cake? I just baked some fresh—let me get you a piece. Ralph took the grandkids with him to the hardware store to buy supplies to build a bat house. Don't ask me why. I've never seen any bats around here, but when those three get something stuck in their heads...

All I know is, whenever Ralph is working on a project with our grandson, Jasper, or our granddaughter, Lark, he looks and acts ten years younger. I think homeschooling our grandchildren these last three years has been as good for us as it has been for them. We've always been very involved in their lives, especially after their mother died almost ten years ago, leaving our son, Nathan, to raise a baby and a toddler.

We are both very proud of the job Nathan has done with these two lovely children. They are very polite, respectful, and mature beyond their years. As you can imagine, it wasn't easy. For years Nathan dropped them off at day care on his way to work. After putting in a full shift, he would pick them up, feed them, bathe them, read to them, put them to bed, and then work into the night cleaning the apartment, paying the bills, and everything else required of a single dad.

To give Nathan a break, Ralph and I usually took the kids on the weekends, but that was all we could do because we were both still working full-time ourselves. Even at that, I ended up using all of my sick days and most of my vacation taking care of Jasper when he would get sick, which was often. We assumed that he was simply picking up every little bug that the other children brought to day care with them. We hoped that things would get better once he entered kindergarten.

Unfortunately things got worse. He developed asthma, which led to the discovery that he was allergic to just about everything in his home and environment. Nathan had to ask his landlord to rip out the carpet in Jasper's room. He bought special sheets and pillows for his bed, and we bought an air purifier for his room.

That helped a bit at home, but school was still the biggest problem. Every kindergarten has to have a class hamster, a pretty teacher's perfume, milk for lunch, and plenty of fresh air and sunshine (which means dust, pollen, and grass). School was a nightmare for Jasper. The allergies made him irritable, and he was constantly getting into trouble. He was taking every conceivable antihistamine, which made it difficult for him to concentrate, resulting in poor grades.

This went on through first grade and into second until it got ridiculous. Runny noses, itchy eyes, and all-night coughing turned into chronic sinus infections. By Christmas vacation Jasper had already missed twenty-one days of school. The infection set into the nasal bones, putting him on antibiotics for three months, and he was constantly sleep deprived. (It's hard to get any sleep when you are coughing all night.) Every time he'd get better, Nathan would send him back to school and Jasper would get sick again.

Ralph and I were planning to take a trip to Georgia over the Christmas holidays, but we decided to postpone that trip and see if we could nurse Jasper back to health. The whole plan was to give his immune system a rest by letting him sleep as much as he needed, cutting back on the decongestants and antihistamines, and stuffing him full of Grandma's home-cookin'. The difference was noticeable almost immediately, and within days he was able to play all day with Lark and sleep peacefully all night.

We all knew the real test would come once he returned to school. Sure enough, by the end of the first week back, the cough had returned along with migraines that progressed to vomiting. It was time to do some investigating at that school. Come to find out that the basement had flooded over the summer and the damage had been painted over.

In our research we also learned that both old schools and new schools can be toxic to an allergic child. Because Jasper's school was an older school in the middle of renovations, he was in double trouble. His little immune system was trying to deal with the mold in his own classroom, the glue in the carpet, and the chemicals in the construction materials.

Ralph and I knew we had to do something to rescue Jasper when he had an asthma attack in the middle of the school day and couldn't find his backpack with his bronchodilator inhaler. The school nurse diagnosed it as croup and called me at work. I immediately asked her to look and see if Jasper's lips were turning gray, if he was having trouble talking, and if it looked like he was breathing from his belly. When she answered yes to all three questions, I very loudly told her to hang up the phone and call 911 immediately.

I rushed to the ER where they already had Jasper hooked up to a steroid IV, got a nebulizer going, and put him on oxygen. What if I hadn't been at my desk to take the nurse's call? Ralph and I spent the next three days while Jasper was in the hospital reassessing our life plans in light of the near loss of our grandson.

We had always talked about retiring early and visiting the Civil War battlefields that Ralph is always reading about, but we never got past the talking stage. We got serious about it this time and decided if we could contemplate retiring early to travel, then we could certainly do it to save our grandson's life.

I gave my notice immediately and began to keep Jasper every day while his father was at work. Ralph needed to stay on through the end of the year before he could receive the benefits we needed. I met with a young woman from our church who I knew homeschooled and asked her my many questions. She was able to answer most all of them, and for those she couldn't answer she offered a big bag of books about homeschooling. I had no idea there were so many resources available! I began homeschooling Jasper within a month. And by the way, Jasper hasn't had another sinus infection or visit to the emergency room since the day he left that school three years ago.

We waited until the next year to have Lark join us. I have always been a little bit uncomfortable with some of the self-esteem exercises they were doing in her class, especially the guided imagery/creative visualization/Twilight Zone mumbo jumbo. It was all a bit too close to mind control for my comfort, but not enough to pull her out of school. Besides, she had learned to read, and I didn't think I could do a better job than what her teacher was doing.

That is until one afternoon when Lark sat down to read her book with Grandpa and he accidentally turned one page too many. She didn't realize it and kept on reading—that is, reading what was on the previous page. Come to find out she had memorized all five of her little school reading books. At that point I realized I *could* do a better job than her teacher because I would have time to pay attention and notice if Lark was really reading or not.

LITERATURE-BASED LEARNING

I had already begun using a wonderful literature-based program called Sonlight to homeschool Jasper. Sonlight is a delightful curriculum that is perfect for grandparents because we typically love to read to our grandchildren anyway. It is my opinion that reading good books is the best way for kids to learn, as opposed to trying to stuff knowledge into them through textbooks. With Sonlight curriculum, history, science, and Bible are taught entirely through literary works.

The best part is being able to teach two grade levels at the same time. Who says that American history must be taught in fifth grade or life sciences in third grade? With this freedom I can teach both Jasper and Lark the majority of their schoolwork together. I schedule individual time with them for math, dictation, and phonics for Lark, but other than that we are one big happy homeschooling family. I've discovered that you really only have to be *one day smarter* than your students, and so far, I've been able to accomplish that.

The heart and soul of Sonlight is the readers. I end up buying most of them because they are so rich, and I find the children reaching for them even when it isn't officially school time. Still, we go through so many books that it can get expensive, and since we are *not* so rich, I find as many as I can at the library. That's not always easy, though, especially if you live in a town with other "Sonlighters," so I keep my eyes open at used book stores, library sales, and (my favorite) garage sales.

The books for each grade all revolve around a single time period in history, so we become saturated in the era. Sometimes we get so wrapped up in the period we are studying that I strike up a conversation with the grandkids as one of the famous historical figures. The other day we were deep into the study of ancient Rome, so I prepared a pseudo-Roman feast for lunch. We were reclining on the floor in our togas and talking as if we were Romans. Lark piped up first. "Oh, I do feel badly for poor Julius Caesar. It was a shame what his friend Brutus did to him," she said casually, as if she were talking about the news of the day. It was so funny that we all started laughing, and I realized that she had learned quite a bit for a small fry.

I handle the history, unless it has to do with the Civil War, in which case Ralph takes over. His other primary responsibility is overseeing all science experiments. What's great is that all of the necessary supplies come with the basic curriculum package, so we don't have to spend half the day assembling everything before getting to the experiment. That's a nice plus.

But the nicest for me is the teacher's manual. I love it because the daily schedule is already made out and there isn't any preparation time, although I still adjust the assignments to fit our needs. I learned early on that I could drive myself nuts trying to cover all the assignments, so I don't feel the pressure to do everything for each grade. Even the creators of Sonlight admit that they have never done all of the assignments suggested in the curriculum. They simply offer a multitude of ideas from which to pick and choose what works best for your family.

You only have to be one day smarter than your students.

I chose to go with the suggested four-days-a-week lesson plan. It works best for us since I have the children year-round anyway, but most importantly because it gives us much more freedom. Some weeks we use Friday for field trips. At other times, if I wake up extra tired or if I'm having a flare-up with my arthritis, I declare a "snow day" and we watch videos together. It's nice to have that extra day built into the week.

One of the ironies about Ralph and I retiring early to homeschool the grandkids is that we are actually getting to do what we always dreamed of doing. We have already taken four trips to study Civil War battlefields. Only this time with the grandkids, Ralph can share it with someone who is *really interested!* Though I must confess it is truly remarkable how the war comes alive when you walk where all those brave young men met their fate.

LESSONS FROM THE FISHIN' HOLE

Oh, and Ralph has found a fishing buddy in Jasper. Together, they figured out a way to go fishing and call it schooling. Last summer they went to the lake on a particularly hot day, and although the boys endured the heat, it was no use—the fish weren't biting for them. Of course, it didn't help that boats all around them were hauling in fish. Finally, they called it a day and headed home.

Jasper stomped all the way to the truck, holding back tears as he watched other fishermen weighing their catches. When he climbed into the pickup, he slammed the door and burst into tears. "It's not fair that I didn't catch a fish when I tried so hard!" he cried.

Ralph offered the standard grandpa answer: "Well, son, it's time you learned that life isn't fair and we don't always get everything we want."

When they returned home, I directed Jasper to the shower before requiring him to write an essay on what he had done that day. I just couldn't justify a day fishing with Grandpa as school unless we had something on paper to show for it. Jasper got out his notebook and markers and asked if he could draw a picture instead. When he was finished he handed me an adorable drawing of an old man and a young boy in a boat with dangling, empty fishing hooks. Underneath was the caption, "Today in homeschool I learned that life isn't fair and you don't always get what you want." Ralph and I both agreed that if he really did learn that lesson, then it was more important than if he had stayed home all day doing long division.

My favorite way to spend a Friday afternoon is building compassion in my grandkids. For years I have helped out at a homeless shelter, and now Jasper and Lark join me as we hand out sack lunches and small bags of toiletries. I'm teaching Lark how to knit, and we are making afghans and booties to bring with us at Christmas. Another special thing we do as a family is making birthday cards for residents at the local nursing home. It was simple enough to get a list of birthdates from the administrative office. And we make a point of hand delivering each card. For many this is the only card they will receive all year, and our delightful young delivery persons never fail to bring a big smile to the residents' faces.

Before I give you an overly idealistic impression of our homeschooling experience, let me assure you that there are days when it looks like we've taken a field trip to the zoo without ever leaving the house. You can't homeschool and expect to have a home that looks child-free, and don't think your children won't act like animals occasionally. And by all means, be realistic.

Realize that I am telling you about some of our homeschooling highlights. I haven't mentioned the fact that I am not a morning person. After Nathan drops the kids off at our house in the morning, I sit them at the breakfast table with cartoons on while I try to wake up a bit. We sometimes don't get school going until after lunch. I have to start slower these days, so the kids help me with the chores, they work with Ralph in the garage, or we bake, which is my favorite form of personal therapy.

I think I mentioned this to you earlier, but I must say it again. Ralph and I have gotten as much out of homeschooling as Jasper, Lark, and Nathan put together. Getting to know our grandchildren so well is a wonderful gift. Peeking into their souls while discussing slavery; gazing at their hearts when they serve a stranger; catching a glimpse of their humor over a board game; watching their understanding awaken when a science experiment works— these are moments when I know I really *do* have the smartest, most talented, cutest grandchildren in the whole world. And I get to spend every day with them!

Chapter Thirteen

The Family Business

S tep into my office. I know it looks suspiciously like a laundry room, but trust me—there's a computer, fax machine, and a printer hidden in here somewhere, probably under a pile of dirty clothes. Please, don't give it a second thought; you're not disrupting a thing. My day rarely runs as planned anyway. You are simply interrupting my interruptions, and I don't mind that a bit.

I hope you don't get whiplash observing our family. We tend to be on the move at all hours of the day and night. That's why we began homeschooling in the first place.

When we moved here five years ago, our lives were turned upside down. Greg's hours were shifted to where he had to leave the house by three-thirty every afternoon, and he didn't return home again until almost one o'clock in the morning. My husband set his alarm clock so he could kiss our four boys good-bye every morning before they headed out the door to catch the school bus, and that was the extent of their time with dad. As the boys got older, it became increasingly obvious that a quick hug (kisses were now out of the question) and an offhanded "Stay out of trouble today" while they were rushing out the door was not going to be enough male influence to guide them successfully through puberty.

Gregory repeatedly appealed to the powers-that-be to get his hours changed, but his boss was not receptive; he made it clear to Greg that he would grant him all the free time he could want if he continued to ask.

Somebody's schedule needed to change so that we could all be together as a family *sometime* during the day, but I never seriously gave homeschooling a second thought. I loved my job, we needed two incomes to survive, and the boys needed to survive adolescence. I was afraid that if I spent my days at home with four rambunctious boys and their raging hormones, there was a distinct possibility that I would kill them—if they didn't kill each other first.

Besides, the boys loved school. They had great teachers, good friends, and passing grades. I didn't understand all the fuss being made about the decline of public education in America. We had a fabulous experience! That is, until we had to move again.

What a difference a school district makes! It wasn't that the new school was dismal or anything; it just wasn't as strong as the one we had left. And there was still the issue of not being home in the daytime when dad was off work. I began doing a lot of school-searching and soul-searching. The deeper I looked, the more I realized that even our fabulous experience had been more about schooling as an institution than an education to prepare them for life.

While researching at the library, I ran across a transcript of John Taylor Gatto's acceptance speech when he was awarded Teacher of the Year in 1990. A couple of things he said got me thinking:

> What can be done? First we need a ferocious national debate that doesn't quit, day after day, year after year. We need to scream and argue about this school thing until it is fixed or broken beyond repair, one or the other. If we can fix it, fine; if we cannot then the success of homeschooling shows a different road to take that has great promise. Pouring the money we now pour into family education might kill two birds with one stone, repairing families as it repairs children.

That stone struck me between the eyes. Our very own family was in disrepair, torn apart by opposing schedules, and I was leaving it up to other people to repair my children! I had to find a way to make our house a home again.

Mr. Gatto went on to say:

> We've got to give kids independent time right away because that is the key to self-knowledge, and we must re-involve them with the real world as fast as possible so that the independent time can be spent on something other than more abstraction. This is an emergency, it requires drastic action to correct—our children are dying like flies in schooling, good schooling or bad schooling, it's all the same. Irrelevant.

There was my answer. It wasn't a case of finding another good school in which to enroll them; it was a matter of providing them with free time to discover their purpose in life and then getting them started as quickly as possible pursuing it. But how could I make this work? I wasn't at all sure, but I knew what *wasn't* working—me! It was time for me to come home and bring the kids with me.

Easier said than done. Money was an issue, as was my inexperience in teaching. So we started slow. The first thing we did was get to know one another again. Now that the kids and I were home during the day at the same time as their father, we all took advantage of uncrowded museums, wide-open hiking trails, amusement parks with no lines, and empty skating rinks. Some of these outings were educational; some were just for fun and spending time with Dad. We made lunch the main meal of the day so we could all sit around the table at the same time, something that hadn't happened since the boys were toddlers.

At first I worried that the children would fall behind in their education during this "exploration period" and I would have to work twice as hard to get them caught up before we could even begin. Instead, the time I took observing each of them, discovering their gifts, and tailoring their days according to their own goals provided the beginnings of a solid foundation on which to build a life education.

Funny. I had wanted to keep the boys in school because I was afraid they would drive me crazy. But the more time we spent together, the more opportunity we had to develop our relationship. We grew to truly respect one another, and that was the key to having them home and making our time together joyful and productive. I knew we had made the right decision when the boys began volunteering hugs and kisses again with no apparent motive.

FAMILY BUSINESS: WE'RE IN THIS TOGETHER

But if this were going to work out, I had to find a way to provide additional income to help Greg, who was already working as hard as he could. I began scouring the newspaper and the Internet for ideas. Unfortunately, I found more work-at-home schemes than anything of real value. There was one exception, a website for work-at-home moms that offered numerous suggestions for viable home-based businesses—bookkeeping, bridal services, business card printing, convention planning, desktop publishing, gift baskets, hairstyling, medical transcription, proofreading, website design, etc. Then there were the more unusual ideas—balloon sculpting, cartoonist, clown, doll design, face painting, ghostwriter, personal shopper, puppy day camp, reminder service, storyteller, and piñata maker.

But I couldn't see myself doing any of those jobs. Our savings were running out and things were about to get desperate when the boys sat me down and gave me a talking-to. They said, "Mom, we're going to ask you the same question you've been asking us for months: What do you want to do with the rest of your life? What floats your boat? What makes you tick and tingle?"

They were right. I had been thinking only about how I could make a few extra dollars, not about how could I live what I loved and make money doing it. So I dug deep and reached for a dream that I had stuffed down since high school: I started a home business designing and selling personalized themed invitations and thank-you notes for children's birthday parties.

What I hadn't counted on was this business growing to the point that it turned into a *family*-run business. *This* is homeschooling in a nutshell to me—a family effort that teaches real-life skills with real life as our classroom. My kids and I have learned everything from budgeting and marketing to production models and web design in the process.

Grab a hold of something so you don't get knocked over in the whirlwind, and I'll tell you about a typical day. I usually wake up around six o'clock and work in the office/laundry room until nine. I'm able to get the majority of my creative work done during that quiet time while the rest of the family sleeps in. Gregory works so late that he needs the extra few hours' rest in the morning, and the boys, well, they're all teenagers now and "require more sleep."

Not that I bought into this line of reasoning without a fight. I thought I was being congenial by allowing the boys to sleep in until seven. After all, I didn't take them out of public school so they could become lazy bums, sleeping their lives away. There are chores to be done, and it's best to get started early. Don't they want to catch that precious worm?

Obviously not, because they sat Gregory and me down over lunch one day and produced reams of research showing that their body clocks were responsible for them staying up until eleven o'clock every night. *Yeah, right,* I thought. *It has nothing to do with the girl on the other end of the phone line, or the pizza party after the ball game, or the book you just can't put down.* Well, not according to the scientific reports they handed us.

The boys also pointed out that these same reports insisted the average teenager needs at least nine hours of sleep to grow and function properly. Wow! Looking back, they often got less than six hours of sleep when attending public school—it's amazing they were able to function much at all. Knowing that I was not going to rework our entire school schedule just so they could get their beauty rest, they quickly followed up with a plan.

I wouldn't tell them this, but they had me sold the moment they proposed hiring a cleaning service to come in once a week. They agreed to allow me to deduct a portion of their weekly salaries to off-load some of the more time-consuming cleaning jobs we were all sharing. They would continue to do all of the laundry and keep the kitchen clean, but everything else would be done once a week by my dear Theresa. Oh, tell me how I got along without her for so many years!

They promised to get up every morning—maybe not bright and definitely not early—at nine o'clock and, after a quick breakfast, immediately begin their schoolwork. We discovered a computer-based homeschool curriculum about the time our second son entered junior high, and it has proven to be perfect for our situation (at least now that we have three computers in the house). Greg handles most math- and science-related questions, and I'm available to help them with the rest of the load. Our youngest likes a lot more hand-holding than the other boys, especially when it comes to studying for the tests (he tends to panic).

I have to discipline myself to let the phone go to voice mail or stop mid-sentence when writing an e-mail if the boys need my help. Believe me, it is a balancing act; but if I'm going to lose my footing going too far in one direction, then I would much rather land on the family side than on the business side. Thankfully, I have found that as the boys get older, they are developing better study habits and becoming more independent learners.

This is homeschooling in a nutshell—teaching real-life skills with real life as our classroom.

Our oldest son, Mark, enjoys his accounting responsibilities in the family business so much that he is continuing his education by earning a college degree on-line. His point was, Why fix something that ain't broke? (I promise, I taught him better grammar than that.) He loves the freedom and flexibility to work at his own pace on the computer, and he is saving tons of money by not attending college on-campus. And he actually has more free time to pursue what he loves. Mark has had a garage band for as long as I can remember, so his afternoon is filled with rehearsals and downloading chords from the Internet.

Which brings me to the next portion of our day. The boys spend two hours completing half of their schoolwork in the morning, tackling their most difficult subjects first. The next two hours we all work together in the business, returning calls, filling orders, making deliveries, processing receivables and payables, brainstorming new themes, designing product, writing ads—you name it. Greg even willingly jumps in occasionally when he's feeling left out.

After a big family meal together, the boys have the remainder of the day to do whatever they like. Samuel works with a neighbor learning the interior trim trade. Jeff wants to be a major league baseball player, so he's practicing, playing, or umpiring a game almost every afternoon. Benjamin likes to design and build ramps and rails for his extreme skating tricks, so he's either on the computer or in the cul-de-sac. Often one or more of them will just hang out with Dad before he leaves for work.

Once the sun goes down, the boys finish up any remaining schoolwork in time for us to gather around the fire and journey together to Narnia, Camden Town, Fleet Street, or some other exotic locale. I hope they never discover that these classics are normally studied for a (gasp!) grade, not enjoyed just because they are great stories. And please don't tell them that children typically outgrow wanting their mother to read aloud to them. That'll be our little secret.

I'm so proud of my boys. They are growing into fine young men, and thanks to the flexibility of homeschooling, Greg and I *both* get to witness and be an integral part of this amazing transformation.

Chapter Fourteen

Life as a Field Trip

D id you have any trouble finding our RV site? We usually ask for a space near the playground area so we can keep an eye on our boys. I hope you don't mind sitting at the picnic table; we like to take advantage of every opportunity to get out and stretch our legs a bit. Our motor home is comfortable, but there's nothing like fresh air.

I'm so glad it worked out that we could meet before we hit the road again. We're singing "On the Road Again" about eight months out of the year, so it is nice to be able to land back in our hometown for a couple of weeks. Of course, our days at home are usually packed with doctor's appointments, hair color touch-ups, seeing old friends, and overnighters at Grandma's house. Then we all start getting the itch to take to the highways again. A family can get spoiled pretty quickly by the simplicity and freedom of the RV lifestyle.

I can't believe it's already been three years since we sold everything, packed up, and headed out on the adventure of a lifetime. Before then, our lives were the epitome of the classic upwardly mobile family. We lived in a beautiful two-story home in the 'burbs with two boys, ages five and seven, and a Yorkie who was eighty-four in dog years.

My husband, Terrell, was spending an average of two hundred days a year traveling from city to city, conducting weeklong seminars for a software company. He grew increasingly tired of the road warrior lifestyle of restaurant meals and solitary nights in hotels. At the same time, Jamal, Lashawn, and I were reaching the end of our ropes trying to make a life without Daddy. We came to a proverbial fork in the road and decided not only to take the highway less traveled, but to make our home on it.

Not that it was that easy. We spent a full year of planning before we could live our dream. The first step was persuading the owner of Terrell's software company that this was also in *his* best interest. Terrell laid out a compelling plan for scheduling multiple seminars in the same region before moving on to the next market. He showed how travel-related expenses could be cut in half by eating at "home" rather than dining out every meal. RV parks cost a fraction of what hotels run. And even a monthly payment on a motor home, plus fuel and insurance, wouldn't come close to what the company was spending on airline tickets for Terrell. There were also the emotional and psychological benefits of being able to come home to his family every night. The boss was convinced.

The next order of business was downsizing—*way* down. I cannot tell you how the cares of the world fly off of your shoulders as you carry out truckloads of stuff to be hauled off to Goodwill. Believe it or not, the boys were able to pare down a roomful of toys to a single box of their favorite things. I was able to whittle a walk-in closet full of clothes into a handful of hangers. Terrell was able to reduce a garage full of tools to a single chest. And we all went from having our own dresser to having our own drawer.

We stored our furniture in my sister's shed, had a blowout garage sale, sold our house, purchased a motor home, and never looked back. Well, there was the time I glanced over my shoulder when both boys were sick with the flu for three weeks. Oh yeah, and I almost turned into a pillar of salt the time it rained for a whole month in Seattle. But most of the time I pinch myself wondering if I'm in a dream or just living one.

We probably couldn't have made this work ten years ago, before the information and communications boom. What we lack in household items, we make up for in office supplies. We don't have a dishwasher in the RV, but we do have a printer/copier/fax machine. No washer or dryer; laundry is done in campground Laundromats. But we have two computers. Oven, blender, vacuum cleaner? Nope. How about two cell phones, a digital television, and satellite Internet service? Sure!

With advances in technology, today traveling by motor home can be a great option for writers, photojournalists, construction workers, salesmen, performers—any job that keeps you on the road more than at home. The very thing that used to drive our family apart—Terrell's work—is now the nucleus that draws us together.

Once we pull into a town that will serve as Terrell's base of operations for the next two to four weeks, we set up camp at a local RV park. Jamal and Lashawn dash off to check out the playground, while Terrell connects all the lines and hoses and I put the little decorations back up on the surfaces to shift the emphasis from *motor* to *home*. Keeping our living area picked up and neat is even more critical when home is only thirty-six feet long. "A place for everything and everything in its place" is my daily mantra.

Within minutes, the boys have usually made a couple of friends and Terrell is talking about his rig with the neighbor from the next space. We have found RV owners to be some of the sweetest folk in the world. Most of them are older and full of wisdom, experience, and stories, which they're eager to share. Jamal and Lashawn have learned about everything from whittling and wartime to harmonicas and hogwash from these substitute grandparents.

Of course, we're still cautious, but thankfully the RV parks are usually small enough to allow us to keep close tabs on the boys. I don't know if it has anything to do with our transitory lifestyle or if the boys would have been this outgoing anyway, but like Will Rogers, they've never met a stranger. They just stroll up to the office and strike up a conversation with the owner of every new campground we visit.

I'm forever catching them "interviewing" the maintenance manager or pool cleaner or gardener. By asking questions, they learn so much before I even get around to teaching them. I once heard someone say, "When you ask questions, teaching is going on. When the child asks questions, learning is going on." I have found that to be particularly true as my boys get older and continue to develop their winsome people skills.

Not that our boys are sentenced to a life surrounded by senior citizens and camp workers; there are always other rug rats running from the swimming pool to the horse-shoes to the playground and back. Last month I overheard the kind of playground conversation that warms a home-schooling mother's heart. The boys were climbing on the monkey bars with a handful of other kids when they all decided to take a trip to outer space. Before the kids decided which planet of the solar system to visit, Jamal described for them the climate and terrain of each one so they would be prepared if they needed to bring a really warm jacket or an extra supply of ice for their Kool-Aid. We had taken a quick trip to the local planetarium the day before, but I was surprised Jamal remembered so much. It seemed to me he was picking at his brother half of the day and in "time-out" the other half. Obviously, he had been paying attention in between the pestering and punish-ment.

Terrell usually has a few days to tour the city with the family before his seminars start, and we have been to some amazing places in our travels. Before we arrive in a city, we've already researched the local sights and culture. We start with the local historical sites, tourist spots, and famous land-marks, but there is so much to see and do in America that we will never run out of new and exciting educational experiences.

> There's so much to see in America, we will never run out of exciting educational experiences.

We each have our favorite things to do. For example, I'm a sucker for the living history museums. I don't know if I was dozing during history class or what, but I had no idea how captivating history could be! The actors who portray characters from our nation's history are often brilliant. The Revolutionary War, the first Native Americans, the homesteaders, the original colonists, pilgrims, and Puritans all come alive for me now—literally.

Terrell is fascinated with factory tours. He loves to see how things are made and how they work. In a pinch, our family now knows how to make a crayon, a guitar, a potato chip, a tube of toothpaste, a car, a glass bowl, and a baseball bat. He also enjoys taking the boys to historical sites and telling them stories about the events that took place there. If the boys show a real interest in a particular place or event, we try to seize on their interest and pick up a book in the gift shop to help them delve deeper into these fascinating places. I love that the boys are learning things like *why* the Civil War happened, instead of simply drudging through the memorization of the dates and names of the various battles.

Lashawn and Jamal also love anything to do with nature. We have a pass to all of the national parks, and we enjoy spending days hiking this beautiful country. We have had the privilege of experiencing the most amazing beaches, mountains, deserts, forests—quite a change from our previous nature experiences in the city park or the backyard.

Last year the boys got wrapped up in rocks. They read books, explored terrain, watched videos, and collected buckets of rocks. Have you seen that old movie *The Long, Long Trailer,* where Lucille Ball picks up rocks from each state until they take over the trailer? That's what it reminded me of. But I knew every pebble was worth it when we were at the beach one day and Lashawn came running over to me yelling, "Mommy, look! It's an igneous rock!" I thought everyone was staring because he was shouting so loud, but then a couple of mothers sitting nearby asked me how old he was. When I told them Lashawn was six, they were shocked. One of the moms called her son over—he was about ten—and said, "Go hang out with that first grader; he could probably teach you a few things." And he did! The boys pulled out their collection of rocks and drew quite a crowd of kids as they explained the differences between sedimentary, igneous, and metamorphic rocks. The highlight of our travels during this time was a visit to Mammoth Cave in Kentucky, where the tour guide was quite impressed with the knowledge of my junior petrologists.

THE CHARLOTTE MASON METHOD

Once Terrell begins his seminars in each city, our sightseeing slows down a bit. The boys and I hunker down and concentrate a bit more diligently on schoolwork. Although because we adhere to the Charlotte Mason method, school is not that different from what we do on any other day. In junior high our studies will get a bit more serious, but at my boys' ages, we still glean most of our lessons from life and "living" books.

Charlotte Mason was an educator in England during the late nineteenth and early twentieth centuries. She had high expectations and an even higher regard for children. She firmly believed in instilling good habits when children are young and trusting them with living books, not sliced-up, lifeless textbooks. She disdained "twaddle," which was her word for the dumbed-down brain candy that schools often feed our children. A few of her buzz words were *copywork, dictation, journaling, picture studies, map reading, nature walks, spelling notebooks,* and *narration.* Do you have time for me tell you about how we incorporate each of the tenets of her educational philosophy into our everyday lives? Great!

First of all, I've already mentioned the phrase "living books." We mainly accomplish this by staying away from textbooks and workbooks and directing the boys to novels and classic literature. From those books I have the boys copy passages, emphasizing attention to detail and careful penmanship. Once they have mastered the paragraph, I dictate it and have them write it again, concentrating on correct punctuation, spelling, and grammar.

I usually choose books that correspond with what we are learning on the road, and their spelling notebooks are filled with corresponding words and phrases. For example, last month we were in Washington, D.C., so they spelled words like *president, government, Capitol,* and *Supreme Court.* And they copied passages from the Declaration of Independence. We also rent and buy many books on tapes, so we have been able to "read" many of the classics as a family.

My boys love Charlotte Mason. She believed that lessons should be kept short, that there's no need for homework, and that afternoons should be kept free for playing, preferably outdoors. She held the conviction that tests and grades were unnecessary as well. The primary reason she could espouse this radical thinking was because of her faith in the power of *narration*.

Narration is simply allowing Jamal to tell me aloud what he has learned. Rather than requiring him to write a book report, which often kills the joy of the story, he stands and recites to me, his dad, or the lady in the RV office what he thinks are the most important aspects of the passage in question. I love knowing what is going on inside his brain. Can you see how allowing him to process all of the information, and then listening to him share it with me, would eliminate the need for grades or tests? I can know instantly what and how much he has digested from each day's lesson.

The remaining foundational principles of this method fall in areas that we cover almost daily without even working at it. Geography and map work are no-brainers on this trip, and physical education is a prerequisite for sanity when you are cooped up in a small space with two wild and crazy boys.

Charlotte's emphasis on picture study finds us visiting the numerous art museums available to us. The boys also listen to a classical selection from a specific composer at night as they fall asleep, thus covering the need to enrich their souls with good music.

Math is put to practice by calculating miles, diesel costs, fuel efficiency, food budgets, and so on. Still, I insist on following a separate math curriculum to make sure the boys are building on concepts in a methodical manner.

The heart and soul of why we adore Charlotte Mason is our common love of nature. Following her example, we all keep our own nature notebooks. The whole family spends long afternoons exploring God's beautiful creation. We sketch pictures of flowers, birds, creepy-crawly things, and anything else we stumble upon. I usually carry a field guide with me so I can offer common names and Latin names to label our drawings.

I adore reading through our old journals and remembering the time and place of a particular discovery. I encourage the boys to write down the feelings that well up inside them as they gaze upon a flower or watch a furry creature or listen to a sparrow. We have recently begun writing short poems about our nature experiences. You can't imagine what it does to my heart to read the tender feelings of my rugged boys.

These notebooks will be a heritage to pass down to my grandchildren and great-grandchildren. In light of this, I recently copied the last stanza of a beloved Robert Frost poem into my nature notebook. I can think of no better way to record this amazing adventure we are privileged to live:

> I shall be telling this with a sigh
> Somewhere ages and ages hence:
> Two roads diverged in a yellow wood, and I—
> I took the one less traveled by,
> And that has made all the difference.

Chapter Fifteen

On the Job Training

Sorry I'm late. Have you ordered yet? Oh, good. When the waiter shows up, would you order a chicken Caesar salad and a water with lemon for me? I'm going to get Thomas situated in that booth over there with his schoolwork. Thanks! I'll be right back.

Okay, I talked to Rebekah and she made it safely to Dr. Miller's. I can relax for a moment. Things have been so much easier since she began working at the veterinarian's office in the afternoon. Not quite so much worry, but still enough to keep me praying.

Rebekah has always been trustworthy for a teenager; but as you can imagine, it was a difficult decision to allow her to stay home and oversee her own schooling while I was at work. Now that she's sixteen and home alone only in the mornings, I feel much less guilt. I already have my eleven-year-old, Thomas, at the office, and I just didn't think I could push my boss to allow me to bring *two* children to work. He has been very gracious to let me set Thomas up in a small empty office in the back. I'm able to teach him on my breaks and during my lunch hour. We have a pretty good routine in place. He knows that if he gets stuck and can't move on, then he is to pick up his book and read until I can help him out. Most of the time he finds a way to figure it out on his own. Just a day in the life of an "officeschooler."

I am constantly amazed at how much my children have matured since we began homeschooling. They have really stepped up to the plate and taken responsibility for their own education and entertainment. It's certainly not my first choice—I would stay home and coddle and nurture them. But I can see the character that is being developed under less-than-perfect circumstances.

My philosophy of life is to focus on the positive rather than dwell on the negative. Believe me, that's not always easy. My kids have been through more tough times in their short lives than I have in my entire adult life. They are stronger for it but at the expense of childhood innocence. Their first blow of reality struck when Rebekah was six and Thomas was two and their father died suddenly of a massive heart attack.

Because I was unexpectedly thrust back into the workplace, in some ways the kids lost their mother and their father at the same time. I had no other choice but to leave Thomas in day care from seven in the morning until six at night. Rebekah was in first grade, but she joined him every day after school. They clung to each other. I didn't think it was possible for them to be any closer aside from being joined at the hip.

All things considered, things were going along smoothly until a wave of violence struck their school two years ago. By the final semester the school had received fifteen bomb threats, a student had pulled a gun on the gym teacher, and a second-grader had been arrested for threatening students with a razor blade. Then things got personal.

Rebekah was leaving school one afternoon when she witnessed a classmate being jumped by two older girls in the parking lot. When Rebekah stepped in to break it up, she was thrown to the pavement and knocked unconscious. When she came to, the bullies were gone and the other girl was lying there bleeding. The school officials were appalled and assured me they were doing all they could to curtail this recent outbreak of violence. Metal detectors and security cameras had recently been installed at all of the school entrances; but I knew that, ultimately, very little could be done to shield my children from the escalation of anger and casual violence rampant among the youth.

My motherly instincts proved sadly on target when two boys from the local high school were gunned down a month later while waiting to board a school bus. Several others were injured, and the tenth-grader who did the shooting then

> **The school could do very little to shield my children from the escalation of violence.**

took his own life. That's the school Rebekah would be attending this year if I hadn't stepped in and taken drastic action to protect my children.

THE SELF-TEACHING METHOD

I immediately withdrew both children from school, and my father flew in from Pennsylvania to stay with them until I could figure out what to do. I immersed myself in

Internet research every night after work. You wouldn't believe how vast the on-line homeschool community is and the overwhelming support you can receive from them. Within days, I was able to narrow my curriculum choices down to three. I finally decided that the Robinson Self-Teaching Method was probably the best way to go in my situation.

I do not agree with all of Dr. Robinson's philosophies, but overall his method has proven to be exactly what our family needed to be able to homeschool while I continued to work full-time. The approach is a bit rigorous and not as much fun and interactive as other homeschooling options; but again, I choose to look on the bright side and thank God that my children are acquiring good study habits that will benefit them for the rest of their lives. And most importantly, they are safe.

The self-teaching emphasis has worked well for Rebekah because she is able to stay home and do her schoolwork. Sure, we had to lay down some pretty strict rules like no TV, no friends over, and don't answer the door unless you hear our secret knock. When we first started, we found it worked best to keep her day highly structured. After I left for work she had about an hour of chores to do. Her schoolwork consisted of two hours of math, a written essay, and after a short lunch break, two hours of assigned reading. This left her the rest of the afternoon to practice her music before starting dinner for me.

A lovely woman gives her cello lessons at our home twice a week. Rebekah is a gifted musician, and her talent has really flourished these past couple of years with the amount of time she is able to devote to practicing.

More recently, Rebekah has started working part-time. What started out as a routine series of shots for our beloved Barney—the half-golden retriever, half-collie, half-senile pooch who shares our home—turned out to be the chance of a lifetime for my daughter. Rebekah has always loved animals and they have always loved her, maybe because they sense a tender soul. The veterinarian, Dr. Miller, noticed immediately the way animals respond to her. But he was even more impressed with her evident maturity beyond her years. He approached me after the appointment and explained that his receptionist had recently left on temporary maternity leave; he wondered if Rebekah would be able to fill in for her in the afternoons for a few weeks.

That was six months ago. Rebekah is still working there and loving every minute of it. I can't believe the amazing transformation of my shy, melancholy daughter into this confident, capable young woman. The only drawback is her newfound ambivalence over whether to pursue her dream of going to Julliard or to attend veterinarian school. I can't imagine that either would be an option for her if we had not chosen to homeschool two years ago.

The Officeschooler

As you can imagine, there have been a few bumps in the road along the way. Not the least of which was the question, *How in the world am I going to homeschool my youngest child and still keep a full-time job?* I nervously approached my boss and explained my apprehension about sending my children back to public school. I then asked if he had any advice as to how I could homeschool and keep my job.

He is the one who came up with the idea of setting up a little office for Thomas. Of course, the arrangement would be on a trial basis and, understandably, hinged on Thomas's ability to get his work done without hindering mine. I don't know what I would do if Thomas weren't such a voracious reader. Although he usually spends about three hours on his core subjects, he still has four hours to fill with reading, sketch work, and building things with his circuit board. He's not really into sports, but I still think it's important for him to get plenty of fresh air and exercise; so we often spend my lunch break walking together or riding bikes in the park. This is the highlight of my day and has really been great for our relationship.

Independent Study Program: Life Support for a Working Mom

We also benefit from the activities that are offered through our homeschool support group. And I do mean all of us, not just Thomas. Our ISP, or Independent Study Program, has been a lifeline for our family. For me it offers a chance to talk with other homeschooling moms and receive the support and encouragement I so desperately need. There is no counting how many times I thought of just giving up when, out of the blue, a friend called me and invited me out for a cup of coffee with a few other frazzled homeschool moms. I don't know if it's the latte or the commiserating, but we inevitably go home convinced that we've made the right choice to take control of our children's education. The fact that our ISP takes care of all of the government paperwork, student files, and immunization records is just a bonus. I can't imagine having to keep up with all of that after a long day at work.

The support group also provides Rebekah and Thomas with a pool of kids from like-minded families with whom to develop healthy friendships. Between holiday parties, graduation celebrations, team sports, and field trips, they have found a group of "classmates" to grow up with.

One of the beauties of homeschooling is the bond that happens between whole families, not just the kids. A few of the homeschooling dads have been very willing to step in and be the male figure that is so necessary in a child's life. And there has never been a time when one family or another has not offered to take my children with them on "official" outings when I wasn't able to get off from work.

Oh, but I love the times when I do get to make those special memories with them. Just last week, our group went on a field trip to an aquarium near the ocean. It was a beautiful Indian summer day, so after the tour a group of us decided to hang out on the beach awhile before returning home. There were probably twenty kids there—a sleeping infant, a toddler taking tentative steps on the sand, preschoolers using cups left over from lunch to build sand castles, older kids burying each other in the sand, and teenagers rolling up their pants legs and daring the waves to soak them.

I sat with the other moms on discarded jackets and blankets dragged from the trunks of the cars, enjoying an unplanned but much needed time of fellowship. Because this was an autumn day in the middle of the week, the beach was empty except for our little group. On the way home we were talking about our field trip and Thomas remarked, "Mom, the only thing I don't understand is why more people weren't out enjoying such a beautiful day. Where was everyone?" We turned the corner and drove past the kids' old school just as their friends were getting out for the day. As Thomas watched the kids streaming from the building, it dawned on my son why the beach had been so empty that day!

At that moment I knew that although we may not have the ideal homeschool situation, my children were safe with me—and it wasn't even a stretch to look on the bright side.

Chapter Sixteen

Going Against the Flow

Hi, I'm Jennifer. Nice to meet you. I hear Lisa has taken you all over meeting her homeschooling friends. We are a diverse bunch, aren't we? Take heart. That means you'll fit right in! Oh, I forgot, you haven't officially decided to homeschool yet, have you? Well, allow me to put my two cents in before you make a decision.

First of all, let me say that I congratulate you for taking the time to research this option so thoroughly before you decide whether to take the plunge. Too often I've seen families barely stick their toe in the water before they declare that homeschooling is over their heads and retreat to the familiarity and comfort of their old deck chairs.

Other parents panic when they discover their children are swimming in shark-infested public school waters, so they pull them out and jump into the deep end of the homeschooling pool without knowing how to swim. As soon as they get that sinking feeling, they climb out and settle for wading in a stream of piranhas. Sure it's dangerous, but they figure a shallow education *feels* so much safer than trying to keep your head above water.

You are very wisely testing the waters before you jump in with both feet. When I was a little girl, every summer we visited my cousin in Florida who had a swimming pool in her backyard. I was always amazed that first thing in the morning, she could run outside, hurtle herself off the diving board, and do a cannonball into the water. No matter how warm it was outside, I was always tentative, taking little steps into the shallow end. I would wade in up to my ankles, and then step down until I was wet up to my knees. Then I would catch my breath as I stepped onto the bottom surface and felt the chill edge up to my belly button. Finally, after my body was somewhat adjusted to the temperature, I would close my eyes, hold my nose, and stick my head under. Within minutes I was frolicking in and out of the water, wondering why the water felt ten degrees warmer than when first I ventured into it.

That is exactly how I waded into the homeschooling waters last year. With my firstborn, Ryan, in kindergarten, this is my first year homeschooling, but I've been doing research on it since he was in preschool. When it came time to enroll him in school, I just couldn't do it. For one thing, I was falling in love with him and my daughter, Ashley, more every day. The thought of enrolling her in day care again and spending another year of their young lives being with them only in the evenings made me heartsick.

What made the choice a bit more complicated is the fact that just the year before, I was named Teacher of the

Year at the public school where I had worked for over a decade. The truth is, as much as I enjoyed being with my children, that wasn't the only reason I chose not to send them to school. As the front page of our local newspaper put it, "When the teacher of the year keeps her kids out of public school, there must be something wrong."

Well, yes, actually there are many things wrong, and sincerely, the least to blame are the teachers. They are under so much pressure to get kids through the program so they can pass the almighty tests—thereby improving the school's statistics and funding—that they can't take the time to help the students enjoy learning. I was always thinking, *My students have to test well so our school can get good scores.*

Our community is growing at a pace that we could build a new school every year and still not have enough room. The result is, even with all the talk of smaller classrooms, our schools continue to burst at the seams. They are piling in the students, which means school is often more about crowd control and standing in lines than it is depth of education.

As a teacher I often felt like I must be more proficient at juggling than imparting knowledge. You put thirty kids in a room and some of them are going to fall through the cracks. Even though the slower students got the majority of my time, I never had enough time to make sure they understood the concept before I had to move on. At the same time, I knew the brighter students were bored, and yet all I could do was give them more busywork, when what I really wanted to do was help them to reach their full potential.

Every teacher knows what every parent of multiple

children says: "Each one of my kids is completely different." Unfortunately, the textbook I taught from was designed for a one-size-fits-all setting. The average student did fine, but contrary to popular opinion, there really aren't that many *average* students. Maybe that's why so many educators end up homeschooling their kids—they don't want to gamble that one of their kids may not be average.

My mother, who has taught first grade for more than thirty years, is the one who first suggested I consider homeschooling. She said, "I've chosen to remain in the public school system. I see it for what it is, and I'm doing my part to make it the best it can be by pouring my life out for my students." At that point she picked up Ashley, her only granddaughter. Then she held my gaze like only a mother can and said, "But, honey, you need to look out for your babies."

Although I had the support of my mother and my husband—did I forget to mention that he is a junior high math teacher?—I had to test the homeschooling waters by swimming upstream. Most of the educators around us knew what was going on in the schools and were very supportive. Quite a few of them have their own children in private schools, so they really don't oppose homeschooling.

"Honey, you need to look out for your babies."

But there are the exceptions who take my decision personally, as if I'm indicting them as educators. I feel terrible about that because there are so many incredibly devoted public schoolteachers. Whenever I get the chance, I pull these defenders of the system aside and explain to them that my decision to leave was not based so much on the negatives of government-run school as much as it was the benefits of teaching my own children. What usually helps them to understand is when I ask them, "What is the number one thing we as educators grumble about?" The answer, of course, is parents not being involved in their children's education. I simply made the choice to become involved *100 percent.* Once they hear it explained that way and realize I'm not calling into question their commitment or success as teachers, the lightbulb is usually switched on. They know as well as I do that parents can teach kids very naturally. Someone with a master's degree cannot get to your child like you, as the parent, can.

Believe me, it isn't my credentials that open the door to my child's heart and mind; it's my unconditional love. Of course, there have been days when Ryan has stretched my patience and I have become as frustrated with him as I was with the fourth graders I taught. The big difference is, Ryan knows that I love him more than any other little boy in the whole world and that there is nothing he could ever do that could change that.

Nonetheless, I was still intimidated about teaching my own child. So I did what any good teacher would do: I went to the library. I checked out every book they had about homeschooling. Then I borrowed all of their homeschooling magazines. While I was there, I used a computer to research as much as I could on the Internet until the librarian kicked me out and locked the doors for the night.

The next thing I did was to call Ellen, a homeschooling mom in our neighborhood. I invited her over and asked her a couple of hundred questions while our kids played together in the backyard. I couldn't believe how much information this innocuous-looking woman had stored up just waiting for a newbie like me to ask her about. Once she realized I was sincerely interested in her experiences and not looking for a way to condemn her choice, Ellen turned into a homeschool evangelist before my very eyes. Before she left, I was converted and shouting right along with her, "Hallelujah! I'm free at last!"

Between Ellen's advice and the abundance of direction I received from my very fruitful trip to the library, I came up with a game plan and was ready to tackle the task of launching our homeschool. My next call was to the Home School Legal Defense Association in Virginia. I asked them to send me a copy of my state's laws regarding homeschooling. They agreed to send them to me but suggested I visit their website if I needed the information sooner.

Next I called the state homeschool association, asking to be put on their mailing list so I could keep abreast of activities available for homeschoolers in my area. They took my address and recommended that I log on to their website for up-to-the-minute information.

I was picking up on a theme here and realized that it would probably be a good idea to have an Internet connection installed. I was so glad I did because if I had waited to receive the newsletter in the mail, I would have missed the home educator's conference that was scheduled for the very next weekend.

Curriculum Fairs and Conventions: Homeschool Heaven

Oh my goodness! How do I even begin to describe the convention experience? Let me start by saying that if you decide to homeschool, make every effort to attend one of these conventions/conferences/curriculum fairs. Whatever they call it in your area, it's worth going to.

The moment I stepped into the building, it seemed to me these homeschooling waters I was testing resembled the Pacific Ocean more than my cousin's swimming pool in Florida. There were *thousands* of moms and dads moving in every direction. I retreated over to a chair in the corner and opened my registration packet, searching for help. I was giddy with excitement. As I glanced over the workshop topics that were available, I found myself wishing there was either more than one of me or more than two days of classes. There seemed to be a seminar addressing every question I had. I got out my yellow highlighter and plotted a schedule.

My neighbor had wisely warned me not to try to do too much on the first day, so I decided to attend three classes, *Homeschooling 101, Discovering Your Child's Learning Style,* and *How to Choose the Curriculum or Method That's Right for You.* I targeted seminars titled *Teaching Your Child to Read, How to Organize Your Home 4 School,* and *Help, I Also Have a Preschooler!* for the second day.

Most of the workshops were immensely helpful. Even so, there was one speaker I did not agree with at all, so I slipped out of her class and caught the end of another one. I learned rather quickly that it's okay to glean the information that works for my situation and toss out the opinions that don't fit my personal beliefs, circumstances, or educational philosophy. The speaker may be an "expert" in her field, but I'm the expert on my family.

In between workshops I visited the exhibit hall—aisles and aisles, rows upon rows, table after table filled to over-flowing with homeschooling supplies and resources. I found every imaginable curriculum, every conceivable method, and every possible resource. It would take me more time and money than I could ever spend to fully familiarize myself with the wealth of materials available to both the beginning and the experienced homeschooler.

It had to be God that the first booth I visited was sell-ing a book written by an author who described, explained, and reviewed the majority of the materials available. I immediately bought the book and once again retreated to my hideaway chair in the lobby. I whipped out my yellow highlighter and marked each of the products I wanted to survey.

Oh, how I wished I had an entire day to spend looking at each and every booth. I recognized that I must set some limits or my spending could very quickly get out of con-trol. The first restraint I put in place was a moratorium on buying anything I had only looked at once. The first pass through the exhibit hall was simply to make notes of booths I wanted to go back and look at more closely on the second pass. I then forced myself to return to my hotel room and thoroughly read through my notes, catalogs, and resource book before making any final decisions. I looked over my workshop syllabus and reviewed what I had learned about Ryan's learning style, then compared that with the teaching method that most closely aligned with my personal goals. Having done my homework, I was ready to return to the exhibit floor and take advantage of the "convention discount" and savings on shipping charges. Wow! It took me a day or two after I got home to come down from the conference high.

This was getting more fun and exciting every day. I was eager to find and join a homeschool support group in my area—that is, after I realized that I was not going to be standing up at each meeting and confessing, "Hi, my name is Jennifer, and I am a homeschooler."[1] Thankfully, we don't sit around in a circle and talk about our problems either. At least not in the one I eventually joined.

These groups come in all shapes and sizes to fit whatever degree of support you are looking for. There are national, state, and local groups. Among the local groups, there are those that are laid-back and those that are uptight; holier-than-thou and live-and-let-live groups; small ones focusing on relationships and big ones concentrating on opportunities; and everything in between.

I chose a large group because I needed all the help I could get. This one offers field trips, park days, sports leagues, graduation ceremonies, newsletters, school plays, clubs, spelling bees, yearbooks, class photos, Moms' Night Out, and much more. The best part is, Ryan and I make new friends every time we show up at the monthly meetings.

At our first meeting, I was able to pick up some record-keeping forms that comply with our state's requirements. On the way home I stopped by the office supply store and bought a simple filing system, and I immediately got to work organizing the relatively small amount of paperwork required. I now have a cumulative file to collect Ryan's records from year to year. I requested a copy of his immunization records from the pediatrician's office to put in another file. I also made a list of the subjects I would teach that year and the materials I planned on using and placed it in a file marked "Course of Study."

I bought a small calendar to record his attendance, which I thought was funny. Should I mark off every day when my little boy hops into bed with me, or does it only count if we've read a book? I figured that Ryan would like the formality of a bona fide report card, so I worked up a homemade one on the computer to insert in the progress-and-transcripts file.

I also bought a fat folder with plenty of room to keep samples of Ryan's work, copies of his art, lists of books he's read, photos from field trips, and such. I figured that this would verify that there was an education happening on the premises. And I just like to keep that kind of stuff anyway.

I later learned that there are complete record-keeping organizers, homeschool daily planners, and software that allow you to simply fill in the blanks. I'm sure these tools would be helpful for a new homeschooling parent, but for me, keeping a few files is a breeze compared to the piles of paper and forms I was used to filling out to keep track of thirty students.

Now that I had our school in order, it was time to concentrate on getting my home organized. That meant decluttering every nook and cranny so that I could fill it up with school paraphernalia. My husband, Clark, built shelves in the kitchen, Ryan's bedroom, the guest room, the hall, and the garage. And it still isn't enough. How in the world have I collected so many books in such a short period of time? You would think I was buying rabbits the way they have multiplied!

I also have a box collection. No, I'm serious. I'm addicted to containers. Small or large, square or rectangle, hinged or open, corrugated or plastic, handled or flat—I love them all the same. I don't play favorites (although I do appreciate the ones I can hang file folders in a wee bit more), and I use each and every one of them. I have one for toys, two for pencils and paper, three for library books and teacher's manuals, four for art materials, and five for school supplies. I know, I'm obsessive. Maybe I should join a support group for boxaholics.

I set up all my supplies in the guest room and transformed it into a one-room school house, complete with desks. That lasted about six weeks. It took me that long to recognize that I was missing out on the advantages of homeschooling by trying to simply make it "school at home." Since we've moved the classroom to the kitchen, the couch, and the park, things have run much more smoothly.

The other thing that has helped calm the waters has been setting goals and making a schedule to reach them. One Saturday morning while Clark took the kids to their play group, I took a trip to the library to clear my head and make a plan for the year. I listed all of the academic goals, character traits, family values, and work habits I wanted to build in Ryan during his kindergarten year.

From that list I was able to come up with a monthly, weekly, and daily schedule. Please don't laugh. It's the teacher in me coming out again—I can't help it.

Every day begins with a regular morning routine including a good breakfast, teeth brushing, and room cleaning. Ryan has a few daily chores to do before it is time to snuggle up in the recliner to read a story from *The Book of Virtues* with both little ones in my lap.

As much as I believe structure is important for our day to be successful, I'm actually very relaxed when it comes to the actual schooling. The majority of our learning is done through arts and crafts, read-a-long books and tapes, science cartoons, and educational videos. To effectively teach a child through second grade, it is really not necessary to allot more than sixty to ninety minutes for official academics. That much one-on-one time goes a long way.

I highly recommend you get a math program with manipulatives like blocks or rods to help turn the abstract concepts into more concrete understanding. I also purchased a phonics program that integrated songs, printing, and easy readers. I get all goose-bumpy just remembering the look on Ryan's face the first time he called his Nana and read a story to her over the phone. In my opinion, next to giving birth, nothing compares to teaching your child to read.

Let me assure you, you *can* do this. If I can do it, you can, too. Does that surprise you that I would make that statement? The truth is, I have come to realize that my teacher training can be a disadvantage in the home environment. Traditional teaching methods still tend to break up learning into several separate categories that are taught independently of one another. It has taken me months to retrain myself to integrate learning into everyday life and not just when we are "doing school."

Will you trust me when I tell you that you will not damage your children for life by homeschooling them? The chance for your child to receive individual attention is, at best, 25-to-1 in a traditional classroom. I'd say the odds are in your favor for producing a successful student. By the way, I want to let you in on a little trade secret about the whole socialization issue. As a public school-teacher I was always telling the students in my class, "Shh! You can socialize when you get home."

So, relax, take a deep breath, and come on in. The water is fine.

1. Carol Moxley, "What's a Support Group, Anyway?" *National Home Education Network*. http://www.nhen.org/newhser/ default.asp?id=294 (accessed December 10, 2002).

Chapter Seventeen

Home Plate

Welcome back to my house. Okay, before we try to digest all we've learned, let's chat over a bite to eat. Have a seat and let me whip up a plate of homemade cookies. Now where is my good knife? Don't you just love a fresh tube of chocolate chip cookie dough? I'll just throw this wrapper away, and we'll be fortified for discussion in eight to ten minutes.

So what do you think about homeschooling now? Pretty exciting, isn't it? Were you surprised at how diverse the families are and how flexible homeschooling can be? I sure hope that our little tour has convinced you that no matter what your situation or limitations, you can find a way to make homeschooling work for you. But...

Believe it or not, I won't be terribly disappointed if our visits have only deepened your resolve that you are just not cut out to homeschool. I think it's good that you know that about yourself. And I admire you for even taking the time to consider the option, even though everything within you was probably screaming, *Oh please, don't make me homeschool!*

On the other hand, that voice may be screaming, *Yes! Yes! This is exactly what I want for my children! Just show me where to go from here.* All right, already. Forget the cookies—let's jump right in!

Keeping in mind that I will give you some more specific direction a little later, let's begin on a more general path. The first thing I suggest you do is buy a couple of good homeschool books or check them out at the library. Make sure you pick up a curriculum resource guide in the mix. From there, do as much research as you can on the Internet. Simply type the word *homeschooling* into a good search engine, like Google.com, then click on the links that look interesting to you. (I don't suggest you begin this if you have supper in the oven or if it's late at night. Believe me, dinner will burn and you will still be surfing when the sun rises.)

Do you know anyone who homeschools? Even if they're only an acquaintance, let me encourage you to invite this person over to your house for a cup of tea and talk. Homeschoolers love to share their passion for their families with others. Don't forget to ask them about support groups available in your area. The more homeschooling friends the better!

You may be able to find out about your state's laws concerning homeschooling from some of your new friends. If not, that information is relatively easy to find. My favorite place to get these kinds of facts is from the Home School Legal Defense Association. They will also be able to assuage any concerns you may still have about homeschooling. This would be a good place to find out the steps you may need to take if you are pulling your children out of a traditional school setting in your area.

The fun really begins when you start looking for curriculum. It helps to have some idea about your children's learning styles. It's also important to note whether a curriculum or method excites you enough to want to teach it. If you have a chance to attend a convention or curriculum fair, then you've got it made. If not, there are so many great Internet sites, books, and catalogs with thorough reviews and descriptions that you will still be able to get a good idea about what will best fit your family.

I hope the families I introduced you to haven't given you the idea that you should only use unit studies if you have a dozen kids. Or that on-line academies are only for the superbusy mom. Or that if your child has ADHD then you should definitely unschool. Mix and match. I know of a mother who teaches her only child with unit studies, an ADHD child who uses the Satellite School curriculum, and a large family that has graduated their children using only traditional textbooks.

Remember, there is no right or wrong way to homeschool. By far the most popular approach is an eclectic one. The more experienced you become as a home educator, the more comfortable you will feel tossing out what doesn't work and trying new things as you get to know your children—and yourself—better. Don't worry, you'll find the *perfect* curriculum for your family—just in time to discover the next perfect method that comes along.

Now it's time to let the adventure begin. Hopefully, your home has a fair amount of discipline and structure in place as a foundation. It is difficult to motivate your kids to do their schoolwork if you have a hard time convincing them to obey you in other matters. If you haven't firmly established your authority in your home, you may want to spend the first few weeks working on this area. I happen to know of a terrific book that may be helpful. Yes, this is a shameless plug for my book *Creative Correction*. But I also sincerely believe it could provide some ideas you may not have already tried in your search for hope, peace, and sanity in your sometimes chaotic home. I'm talking from firsthand experience here.

So what do you want your homeschooling day to look like? Do you plan on beginning with chores? family or personal devotions? cartoons? breakfast? Make a schedule. Even if you have decided to unschool, there are still certain things that must be done every day. Granted, if you are anything like me, your schedule will shape-shift a dozen or so times before you toss it out completely and come up with a more realistic plan. But it's still a good idea to think about where you are going and how you are going to get there.

Remember, you need to relax and enjoy your children.

Even so, I don't think I can stress enough the need to relax and enjoy your children. I know that it is so easy to get caught up in making sure they get all their work done and have plenty of opportunities for socialization and still stay on top of character and behavioral issues—all while attempting to keep a clean house, a happy spouse, and some semblance of order.

Trust me, you are going to be able to pour more into

your children in one good hour than someone else can having them all day long. Especially when your child is young. You may feel guilty about letting the kids play all day while you run after the toddler and the baby, but don't. Try to fit in a bedtime story, count a few M&M's, and sort some laundry together. And then go to bed feeling good about what you accomplished that day.

And don't forget nap time! They need it and you need it. We are the famous napping house in our neighborhood. I still have my kids rest, read, or sleep almost every afternoon. And I'm a better mother and teacher when we get up. We also put the kids to bed earlier than most of their friends. We allow them to stay up and read in their beds or listen to an audio tape awhile, but Steve and I covet our hour or two alone in the evening. I may sound like a really mean mommy, but ever since they were tiny, I have required them to stay in their rooms in the morning until the little hand on the clock points to the seven. This allows me to have my quiet time before hearing the little pat of footie pajamas bearing down on me at the crack of dawn.

Another way to take care of yourself, and hence, take better care of your kids, is to ask for help. Please don't try to do it all. As a matter of fact, is there any way you can clip some coupons or have a garage sale or save some Christmas money to hire a cleaning crew every once in a while? This is not being indulgent; it's being realistic about your time and your inability to be all things to all people. At the very least, involve your children as much as possible in the upkeep of the house. Little ones love to help, and older ones actually *do* help.

I have discovered that as my children have gotten older, homeschooling has gotten easier in many ways. Sure, the schoolwork is tougher, but they are becoming more independent at the same time. And just because they are in junior high or high school doesn't mean that time for relaxation is still not an important priority. Downtime is probably when they will discover what they want to do with the rest of their lives. Never forget that, regardless of age, learning happens all day long, not just when doing official schoolwork.

So relax, trust your instincts, enjoy your children, and have fun!

One Loafer In, One Loafer Out

Hey, I'm so glad you called! I was just thinking about you the other day. A lot has happened since we last talked. We moved from California to Texas, I officially have teenagers, and one has already started high school. Yikes! Life is happening way too fast. By now I'm sure it won't surprise you that although we're still heading toward the same destination on our homeschooling adventure, we're taking a new path to get there.

Our first year in Texas was a bit rough for Tucker, Haven, and Clancy. They grew up in California and had known most of their friends since the playpen. We moved into our new house and immediately started up again with the Alpha Omega *Switched-On Schoolhouse* software program. We love this computer curriculum for homeschooling, but without any friends the kids felt isolated and lonely, stuck in their rooms all day with their faces glued to a laptop monitor.

We discovered a local homeschool support group, and this helped tremendously! By the end of the school year, we had established a healthy schedule that included field trips, babysitting, co-op opportunities, neighborhood fun, Konos classes, and sleepovers. I started a MomTime group in my home and made some friends, and we found a growing church with a phenomenal youth ministry where the kids made new friends.

When I mentioned to people in our community that we homeschooled, many of them asked, "Oh, do you go to the homeschool academy in town?" I didn't even know there *was* such a thing! I visited the school website and grew very excited. Their mission statement proclaimed that their goal was "to educate youth in a historic Christian worldview through a rigorous classical curriculum."

This was pretty much Greek to me.

I found out later it was closer to Latin.

Translation: I had stumbled onto a "best of both worlds" homeschool experience. Two days a week my children could learn from qualified teachers passionate about their subjects and teaching from a time-honored and Christ-centered foundation.

Every other day I would oversee Tucker, Haven, and Clancy's schoolwork at home while continuing to train them up in the ways of the Lord in the everyday challenges and lessons of life. Fridays would be free to use for additional homework time, field trips, fine arts instruction, athletics, or extracurricular activities.

I must admit that, in my excitement, I went a little overboard, signing them up for virtually every opportunity the school offered. I registered Tucker for football, basketball, baseball, classical guitar, and choir. Haven was on the volleyball, basketball, and softball teams and in drama and chorus. (She drew the line at wind ensemble.) Clancy, who isn't much into sports, was very excited about her Friday schedule of voice, drama, and art.

That was before our orientation meeting with the school principal.

We were shocked to learn that the kids would most likely have between one and two hours of homework for every hour of class time. Whoa! I quickly unenrolled them from nearly every nonmandatory class.

Keeping the stress level at a minimum is a high priority for me. Simplifying the extracurricular activities was the first order of business. But I also implemented some other drastic measures in my quest to maintain a peaceful home environment. On days when they go to the school, nobody is allowed to do homework. Kids need play time to let off steam and chill time to simply relax.

After a quick snack when they get home, Tucker, Haven, and Clancy usually run out the door to find a friend, "veg out" in their rooms, or head to the garage to practice the guitar, bass, or drums. We try to reserve weeknights for dinner around the table, with the exception of Wednesday night youth group, which doubles as "date night" for Steve and me. (Don't worry, we're not ditching church; we don't have midweek services.)

At night, before the lights go out, I visit each child for "window time." This is the highlight of my whole day as I sit on the edge of their beds for an extended time and just talk about whatever is on their minds and in their hearts. I don't know if it's the night sky or the lateness of the hour or the pj's, but I have discovered that this period before bedtime is often the window to my children's souls.

It's during these special times I have learned that as much as we love this new homeschool situation, it isn't perfect. The academics are rigorous, and it has been quite a struggle, especially for Tucker. He is very smart, but sitting still in a class, paying attention to lengthy lectures, keeping up with the homework, handling the pressure of midterms, stifling a wisecrack, and parsing Latin have definitely taken their toll. Sometimes it comes out in an angry outburst or flood of emotion, but it is obvious that Tucker keeps a lot of stress barely under the surface just waiting for window time to let it all out. We talk about it and pray about it, and then I go into my bedroom and talk and pray about it some more. Is the load too heavy? Should we try medication? Should I pull him out of school? Have I made a mistake?

On other nights it's Haven that makes me question the wisdom of our course. Especially during those conversations I have with her when she's learned something at school that I didn't send her to school to learn. You know what I'm talking about. Those "lessons" I'd like to shelter her from forever if I could. I know she will find out about the more worldly sides of the world soon enough, but do I really want to pay money to send her somewhere she can learn them even earlier?

And yet most of my doubts come when I'm talking to Clancy. I've always felt like the most important time to homeschool is during the junior high years when children are trying to figure out who they are and how they fit into this world. I want to be the one who helps my child make these discoveries rather than leaving it up to their peers. Kids can be especially cruel at this age, even so-called friends.

Clancy has spent many a window time crying in my arms. One night she bared her heart to me, declaring, "Tucker is the most popular boy in high school, Haven is the most popular girl in the whole school, and me...me? What happened?!" Oh, the agony of puberty!

These are the times when I most miss full-time homeschooling and wonder whether I've made the right decision. Fortunately, when I look back over the years, I must admit that I've felt this way every school year for different reasons. Questions, doubts, insecurities, thinking I'm not cut out for homeschooling, and wondering if I'm really up to the challenge. I've learned to chalk it up to the fact that, as mothers, we will probably always feel like we're juggling too many balls and must reconcile ourselves to the fact that we are going to drop a few along the way. And that's okay. There's no such thing as a perfect choice; there will be trade-offs. The big question is, Do I believe the sacrifices are exceeded by the advantages?

When it comes to our homeschool choice this year, the benefits have far outweighed the few weepy window times. Even what initially looked like negatives have turned into life-preparing positives. At the beginning of the school year, the children's study skills were atrocious. (Who *was* their teacher anyway?) Between a newly acquired study skills curriculum, a tutor, and lots and lots of practice in the classroom, they have become excellent students.

Weekly quizzes, quarterly midterms, and finals have taught them how to study successfully for tests. Multiple homework assignments and long-term projects with a variety of due dates have taught them how to diligently organize their time and paperwork. Having official grades and report cards has proven a wonderful leverage for threats...uh, I mean, *incentives* to retain privileges and develop self-discipline.

I love the fact that somebody other than me is evaluating their creative writing, essays, reports, and other assignments. It's often been difficult for me to take off my "Mother" hat, and so I tended to believe all of their work was brilliant. Writing was one subject I felt especially unqualified to teach. (Go figure.) Weekly writing assignments this year have helped them to flourish in creativity, spelling, grammar, and substance.

I'm confident that the practice they are getting in note taking, time management, taking tests, debating, researching, hypothesizing, experimenting, even taking Latin, will help make the transition from high school to college virtually seamless. In the meantime, they are generally enjoying the whole "going to school" scenario.

Tucker, Haven, and Clancy love to get up and go to class. (Well, Tucker hates the getting up part, but once he's out of the shower, he's nice again.) They have thoroughly enjoyed home-field games, team spirit, lunchtime horseplay, yearbook preparation, study hall antics, school pictures, school plays, and the many other experiences unique to school.

I'm also enjoying their time at school. When the kids are gone, I retreat to our motor home to work and write, while Steve gets caught up on office work at home. Once a week we'll sneak off for a quick lunch, just the two of us. I'm also able to schedule any doctor's appointments, grocery trips, and other errands while they are away. Steve is thrilled because for the first time in our marriage, I'm getting a professional manicure. (Pretty nails have been a thing of the past since baby number two came along—I gave an appointment up in exchange for a nap and never rescheduled.)

I'm even finding that I love the little things, like preparing lunches and driving the kids to school. Early in the year we withdrew from the carpool network because I missed praying with the kids on the way to school, and because I was jealous of the mom who got to pick them up from school and hear all about their day. (We all know that teenagers usually resort to mumbling and one-syllable answers once they step foot in the house.)

On homeschooling days we still have the luxury of beginning the day at a more leisurely pace with family prayer, reading aloud from a good book, doing chores, and playing the occasional game. And with only two days of school a week, we can still travel together when the opportunity presents itself.

For our family, at this time in our lives, the home-school academy has been a real answer to prayer. I love having my kids at home the majority of the time, but twice a week I love seeing them spread their wings and venture out of the nest on test flights.

Where Do I Go from Here?

Or, Let's Take a Look at That Appendix

I promised to give you a little more specific direction on where to begin your homeschool adventure. I've compiled a list of some of my own favorite books and resources to get you started. This is certainly not an exhaustive list. Why not? For one thing, I don't want to overwhelm you right off the bat. But the main reason is that I will only suggest resources that I can, with conviction, feel good about. That means I have either personally used everything listed here or I have a friend who can vouch for it. These recommendations are here simply to give you an idea of what is available. And many of these will lead you to additional books, curricula, websites, support groups, and other resources that may appeal to you.

I also have included a homeschooling section on my website at www.LisaWhelchel.com. As I discover great new products, websites, or other homeschool helps, I will post these finds for you to check out. You will soon realize that becoming a homeschooler means you instantly have thousands of friends who want to share their ideas with you. Consider me your first homeschooling buddy.

General Homeschool Resources

You will find links to each of the following resources at:
www.lisawhelchel.com

Books About Homeschooling

Dumbing Us Down: The Hidden Curriculum of Compulsory Schooling
John Taylor Gatto

The Homeschooling Book of Answers
Linda Dobson

Homeschooling for Dummies
Jennifer Kaufield

Homeschooling for Excellence
David and Micki Colfax

Homeschooling for Success
Rebecca Kochenderfer and Elizabeth Kanna

A Survivor's Guide to Home Schooling
Luanne Shackelford and Susan White

Curriculum Guides

The Big Book of Home Learning
Mary Pride

Christian Home Educators' Curriculum Manuals
Cathy Duffy

Home Learning Year by Year
Rebecca Rupp

HOMESCHOOL MAGAZINES

Home Education Magazine
P.O. Box 1083
Tonasket, WA 98855
(800) 236-3278
www.home-ed-magazine.com

Homeschooling Today
P.O. Box 436
Barker, TX 77413
(281) 492-6050
www.homeschooltoday.com

Practical Homeschooling
Home Life, Inc.
P.O. Box 1190
Fenton, MO 63026-1190
(800) 346-6322
www.home-school.com

The Teaching Home
P.O. Box 20219
Portland, OR 97294
(503) 253-9633
www.teachinghome.com

Homeschool Resource Catalogs

The Always Incomplete Resource Guide
Lifetime Books and Gifts
3900 Chalet Suzanne Drive
Lake Wales, FL 33859-6881
(863) 676-6311
www.lifetimebooksandgifts.com

Christian Book Distributors
(800) 247-4784
www.christianbooks.com

The Elijah Company
1053 Eldridge Loop
Crossville, TN 38571
(888) 235-4524
www.elijahco.com

Timberdoodle Company
E. 1510 Spencer Lk. Rd.
Shelton, WA 98584
(360) 426-0672
www.timberdoodle.com

On-line Resources About Homeschooling

A to Z Home's Cool
www.gomilpitas.com/homeschooling

Homeschooling at About.com
www.homeschooling.about.com

Home School Legal Defense Association
www.hslda.org

Homeschool World
www.home-school.com

National Home Education Network
www.nhen.org

Your Virtual Homeschool
www.homeschool.com

On-line Schools

Alpha Omega Academy
300 N. MeKemy Ave.
Chandler, AZ 85226
(800) 682-7396
www.aop.com

Homeschooling Curriculum and Resources

Art

Child-Size Masterpieces
Parent Child Press
P.O. Box 675
Holidaysburg, PA 16648-0675
(866) 727-3683
www.parentchildpress.com

Draw-Write-Now
Barker Creek Publishing, Inc.
P.O. Box 2610
Poulsbo, WA 98370-2610
(800) 692-5833
www.barkercreek.com

How Great Thou Art Publications
P.O. Box 48
McFarlan, NC 28102
(800) 982-3729
www.howgreatthouart.com

Auditory Learners

Audio Memory
501 Cliff Drive
Newport Beach, CA 92663
(800) 365-7464
www.audiomemory.com

Bible Memory

Awana
www.awana.org

Hide 'Em In Your Heart Songs (CDs and cassettes)
Steve Green

Logos Bible Software
www.logos.com

Memlok Bible Memory System
420 Montwood
La Habra, CA 90631-7411
(800) 373-1947
www.memlok.com

Character Building

Adventures in Odyssey (audio tapes)
Focus on the Family
8605 Explorer Drive
Colorado Springs, CO 80995
(800) 232-6459
www.family.org

The Book of Virtues
William Bennett

Doorposts
5905 S.W. Lookingglass Drive
Gaston, OR 97119
(503) 357-4749
www.doorposts.net

Family Nights Tool Chest series
Kurt Bruner and Jim Weidmann

The Adventures of Patch the Pirate
P.O. Box 6524
Greenville, SC 29606
(800) 467-2824
www.patchthepirate.org

The Charlotte Mason Method

A Charlotte Mason Companion
Karen Andreola

A Charlotte Mason Education
Catherine Levison

Charlotte Mason Study Guide
Penny Gardner

For the Children's Sake
Susan Schaeffer Macaulay

The Classical Approach

Classical Homeschooling Magazine
P.O. Box 873
Morton, WA 98356
(800) 331-6071
www.classicalhomeschooling.com

Trivium Pursuit On-line
www.triviumpursuit.com

The Well-Trained Mind:
A Guide to Classical Education at Home
Jessie Wise and Susan Wise Bauer

COMPUTER-BASED CURRICULUM

Switched-On Schoolhouse
Alpha Omega Publications
300 N. McKemy Ave.
Chandler, AZ 85226
(800) 622-3070
www.aop.com

Robinson Self-Teaching Curriculum
3321 Sesame Drive
Howell, MI 48843
www.robinsoncurriculum.com

CREATIVE WRITING

Any Child Can Write
Harvey S. Wiener

Writing Strands
National Writing Institute
624 W. University, #248
Denton, TX 76201-1889
(800) 688-5375
www.writingstrands.com

EDUCATIONAL GAMES

Aristoplay
www.aristoplay.com

GeoSafari
www.edin.com

GRAMMAR

Easy Grammar and Daily Grams
P.O. Box 25970
Scottsdale, AZ   85255
(800) 641-6015
www.easygrammar.com

Shurley English
www.shurley.com

Simply Grammar
Edited by Karen Andreola
Charlotte Mason Research and Supply
P.O. Box 758
Union, ME 04862
www.charlottemason.com

HANDWRITING

A Reason for Handwriting
Concerned Communications
(800) 447-4332
www.areasonfor.com

Getty-Dubay Italic Handwriting
Continuing Education Press

Portland State University
P.O. Box 1394
Portland OR 97207
(866) 647-7377
www.cep.pdx.edu

Handwriting Without Tears
8001 MacArthur Blvd.
Cabin John, MD 20818
(301) 263-2700
www.hwtears.com

HISTORY

Animated Hero Classics videos
NestFamily
www.nestentertainment.com

Beautiful Feet Books
139 Main Street
Sandwich, MA 02563
(508) 833-8626
www.bfbooks.com

God's World Newspapers
P.O. Box 20001
Asheville, NC 28802-8201
(800) 951-5437
www.gwnews.com

Greenleaf Press
3761 Hwy. 109 North
Lebanon, TN 37087
(800) 311-1508
www.greenleafpress.com

Richard "Little Bear" Wheeler videos and
audio books
228 Still Ridge
Bulverde, TX 78163
(830) 438-3777
www.mantlemin.com

Independent Learning

Alpha Omega LIFEPACS
300 N. McKemy Ave.
Chandler, AZ 85226
(800) 622-3070
www.aop.com

Accelerated Christian Education
8200 Bryan Dairy Rd., Suite 200
Largo, FL 33777
(727) 319-0700
www.schooloftomorrow.com/homeschool

Languages

Artes Latinae
Bolchazy-Carducci Publishers
1000 Brown Street
Wauconda, IL 60084
(847) 526-4344
www.arteslatinae.com

The Learnables series
International Linguistics Corporation
12220 Blue Ridge Blvd., Suite G
Kansas City, MO 64030-1175
(800) 237-1830
www.learnables.com

Power-Glide Foreign Language Courses
1682 West 820 North
Provo, UT 84601
(800) 596-0910
www.power-glide.com

Literature

Books Children Love
Elizabeth Wilson

Honey for a Child's Heart
Gladys Hunt

The Read-Aloud Handbook
Jim Trelease

LITERATURE-BASED CURRICULUM

Sonlight Curriculum
8042 South Grant Way
Littleton, CO 80122-2705
(303) 730-6292
www.sonlight-curriculum.com

The Classics
The Helping Hand
P.O. Box 496316
Garland, TX 75049
(800) 460-7171
www.classicshome.com

The Prairie Primer
Cadron Creek Christian Curriculum
4329 Pinos Altos Rd.
Silver City, NM 88061
www.cadroncreek.com

MATH

CalcuLadder series
The Providence Project
14566 NW 110th St.
Whitewater, KS 67154
(888) 776-8776
www.providenceproject.com

Chalk Dust math video programs
11 Sterling Ct.
Sugar Land, TX 77479
(281) 265-2495
www.chalkdust.com

Five Minutes A Day! Math series
Susan C. Anthony
Instructional Resources Company
www.susancanthony.com

Key To... series
Key Curriculum Press
1150 65th St.
Emeryville, Ca 94608
(800) 995-MATH
www.keypress.com

Math-U-See
(888) 854-MATH
www.mathusee.com

Saxon Publishers
2600 John Saxon Blvd.
Norman, OK 73071
(800) 284-7019
www.saxonpublishers.com

The Principle Approach

The Noah Plan
Foundation for American Christian
Education
P.O. Box 9588
Chesapeake, VA 23321-9588
(800) 352-3223
www.face.net

Reading and Phonics

Alpha-Phonics
Sam Blumenfeld
www.alpha-phonics.com

The Bob Books series
Bobby Lynn Maslen

Sing, Spell, Read & Write
(800) 526-9907
www.pearsonlearning.com/singspell/

Teach Your Child to Read in 100 Easy Lessons
Siegfried Engelmann, Phyllis Haddox, Elaine
Bruner

SCIENCE

Apologia Educational Ministries
1106 Meridian Plaza, Suite 220
Anderson, IN 46016
(888) 524-4724
www.highschoolscience.com

Backyard Scientist books
Jane Hoffman

Considering God's Creation
Eagle's Wings Educational Materials
P.O. Box 502
Duncan, OK 73534
(580) 252-1555
www.eagleswingsed.com

Kids Discover magazine
149 Fifth Ave
New York, NY 10010
(212) 677-4457
www.kidsdiscover.com

SPELLING

Spelling Power
Beverly L. Adams-Gordon

Wordly Wise series
Kenneth Hodkinson
Educators Publishing Service
31 Smith Place
Cambridge, MA 02138-1089
(800) 435-7728
www.epsbooks.com

TRADITIONAL TEXTBOOKS

A Beka
P.O. Box 18000
Pensacola, FL 32523-9160
(800) 874-3592
www.abeka.org

Bob Jones University Press
Greenville, SC 29614
(800) 845-5731
www.bju.edu/press

Calvert School
105 Tuscany Rd.
Baltimore, MD 21210
(410) 243-6054
www.calvertschool.org

Unit Studies

Advanced Training Institute International
Box One
Oakbrook, IL 60522-3001
(630) 323-2842
www.ati.iblp.org

Five in a Row
P.O. Box 707
Grandview, MO 64030-0707
(816) 246-9252
www.fiveinarow.com

How to Create Your Own Unit Study
Valerie Bendt

KONOS Character Curriculum
P.O. Box 250
Anna, TX 75409
(972) 924-2712
www.konos.com

The Weaver Curriculum
Alpha Omega Publications
300 N. McKemy Ave.
Chandler, AZ 85226
(800) 622-3070
www.aop.com

Unschooling

Better Late Than Early
Raymond and Dorothy Moore

Unschooling: Delight-Driven Learning
www.home-educate.com/unschooling

Video Schooling

A Beka Academy
P.O. Box 18000
Pensacola, FL 32523-9160
(800) 874-3592
www.abeka.org

HomeSat
Bob Jones University
1700 Wade Hampton Blvd.
Greenville, SC 29614
(800) 739-8199
www.bju.edu

Standard Deviants Video series
www.cerebellum.com

Workbooks

Frank Schaffer Publications
www.mhteachers.com

Learn at Home series
American Education Publishing, editors

Super Yearbooks
ESP Publishers, Inc.
1212 N. 39th St. Suite 444
Tampa, FL 33605
(813) 242-0655
www.espbooks.com

SPECIAL TOPICS OF INTEREST TO HOMESCHOOLERS

BUDGET HOMESCHOOLING

Cheapskate Monthly On-line
www.cheapskatemonthly.com

Christianbook.com
www.christianbook.com

Homeschooling on a Shoestring
Melissa Morgan and Judith Waite Allee

Homeschool Your Child for Free
LauraMaery Gold and Joan M. Zielinski

Miserly Moms
www.miserlymoms.com

Used Curriculum

Homeschooler's Curriculum Swap
www.theswap.com

Vegsource Homeschool
www.vegsource.com/homeschool

Finding Local Support Groups

Home Education Magazine
www.home-ed-magazine.com

Homeschool World
www.home-school.com

Jon's Homeschool Resource Page
www.midnightbeach.com/hs

Learning Disabilities

NATHHAN
(special needs, disabled, or adopted children)
National Challenged Homeschoolers
Associated Network
P.O. Box 39
Porthill, ID 83853
(208) 267-6246
www.nathhan.com

Learning Styles

Discover Your Child's Learning Style
Mariaemma Pelullo-Willis and Victoria
Kindle Hodson

The Way They Learn
Cynthia Ulrich Tobias

Pre-Homeschool Teaching Resources

Slow and Steady Get Me Ready
June R. Oberlander

Favorites from the Field

I think you can tell by now that I just love talking to other parents about homeschooling. Don't get me wrong; I've read some very informative books on the subject and I continue to scour the Internet for quality resources. But I still get my most helpful support and advice from other homeschoolers.

Maybe the best way for you to learn about all the great homeschooling resources available today is to hear from other homeschooling families. I, being a natural born leader (a.k.a. bossy), will direct the conversation and get it rolling. "So let's go around the circle and each of us introduce ourselves and share what we consider to be our favorite homeschooling resource and why. Don't forget to add where our new friend here"—that's you—"can go for more information."

WHOLE CURRICULA

"Hi, my name is Myrna and I like Accelerated Christian Education for all subjects, except math. It is simple and easy for my children to follow, with minimal background/study for me. It covers everything and includes great character-building cartoons and instruction." *www.aceministries.com/homeschool*

"My name is Mary and I have loved My Father's World curriculum for everyone from kindergarten to eighth-graders. It is chronological and takes you from learning about missionaries and countries to learning about our world from a Christian worldview, from Creation to the present." *www.mfwbooks.com*

"I'm Denise and this is only our second year homeschooling, so we are newbies, too. We have a fourth-grade son with ADHD. Last year we started with Alpha Omega *Lifepacs* and they were good; however, this year we used Alpha Omega's *Switched-On Schoolhouse*, which has basically the same info as *Lifepacs*, except it's all on the computer. This has been *great* for a kid with ADHD, and he is also able to work independently." *www.aop.com*

"I love that program, too! Oh, sorry, my name is Stephanie. I am sooooo excited about the *Switched-On Schoolhouse* curriculum. My daughter is 13 and in the eighth grade. My husband has been deployed to Iraq, and I was about to rip out my hair last year. Now the grades are all figured, the assignments made, and all is well! It takes much less out of me, and her results have been better. You can set up and control all the details you want. It is available many places but I purchased mine from Christian Book Distributors." *www.cbd.com*

"Hello, I'm Joanne. I love A Beka Academy Program 2 on DVD because my kids love it! I love the freedom it gives me. The teachers are so much more creative than I am. It is amazing—my kids even do the drill work and answer questions presented in class by talking to the TV. It is hilarious! I can't say enough about it. My kids said they didn't want me to teach them any other way, they enjoy it so much." *www.abekaacademy.org*

"My name is Christy and, without a doubt, I highly recommend our *Five in a Row* curriculum. It has provided the most fun and wonderful memories for our whole family. I can't imagine homeschooling without it. Plus, *Mom* has learned so much!" *www.fiveinarow.com*

"Hi, my name is Kristen, and this is the second year we have used the K12 program. It is a public school that is government funded; however, I, the parent, get to keep my children home and teach. The Virtual Academy program provides everything for us, from a personal computer and printer down to the paintbrushes. We are very excited about this program that was founded by William Bennett." *www.k12.com*

"I'm Karen and I have four children: a first-grader, a fourth-grader, an eighth-grader, and a preschooler. We love Sonlight Curriculum, mostly because it is literature based. I love reading, and my children love reading. (My reluctant reader has since become a convert and insists she can't get to sleep at night unless she reads for a while!) The way history is taught through 'living books' is very appealing to our family and is a good fit. The second reason I love it is because of the wonderful instructor's guide. When I opted to homeschool, I felt completely and totally inadequate. I literally did not have a clue where to start. I knew that workbooks would burn us out worse than we already were, so the literature method was our curriculum of choice. But *how* do you do it? You follow the instructor's guide, of course! It was wonderful to have everything laid out for me, lots of information for discussion, and questions to ask. I can pick and choose what I want to do, instead of sitting there with my child staring at me while I'm thinking, *What do I do now?* It's wonderful for a first-timer, and it gave me tremendous confidence that I could teach my child." *www.sonlight.com*

"Hi, I'm Lori and I have loved using the Calvert School curriculum. I would recommend this to anyone looking for a complete classical/traditional program. Calvert's lesson manuals are a homeschool parent's dream come true! I now have more time for fun and spend less time planning and searching for 'the perfect curriculum.'" *www.calvertschool.org*

"My name is Joan and we use the Pennsylvania Cyber Charter School. We didn't want our kids subjected to the stuff in public schools, and yet we failed miserably at using public school materials to homeschool our kids. For the last three years we have used this cyber school, and we love it. *www.wpccs.com*

UNIT STUDIES

"I'm Melanie, and we love the Weaver unit study curriculum for so many reasons, I don't know where to begin. Number one: It has been so easy for me to use with both of my children, even when I was new to homeschooling and scared to attempt unit studies. Number two: It covers several chapters from the Bible, incorporating numerous subjects (science, social studies, health, language arts, and others). Number three: The teacher's guide is laid out in a in a step-by-step process, telling you exactly what supplies you need, what you need to do, and often telling you exactly what to say. Number four: It is a three-day-per-week format, which works well, especially for younger children. This made easing into homeschooling less intimidating or overwhelming. Number five: My kids love the things we study and love my learning along with them. Number six: It is easy for me to tailor it to my needs if I don't want to do everything the program suggests or want to add something or need to take a break for family matters." *www.aop.com*

"Hi, I'm Tamara, and I would like to recommend *America: An Integrated Curriculum* written by Chris Roe of Christian Novel Studies. I like it because it is a complete unit study that combines fascinating, engaging literature with American history. There is an emphasis on looking at American history with a biblical worldview, and our children have retained many details because they weren't just memorizing names and dates. Of all the products we have used in over five years of homeschooling, this is my favorite—because it's my family's favorite! *www.christiannovelstudies.com*

"My name is Darci and I love the Konos unit studies. I recommend it because it is so much fun for the kids. They get to play while they learn. They remember more as they are doing activities that reinforce what they are learning." *www.konos.com*

"Hello, my name is Martha and I have been homeschooling my twelve children for thirteen years. One of our favorite resources is the Learning Adventures history-based unit study, beginning in ancient Egypt. All subjects are covered with the exception of math. It comes complete with library book lists and comprehension questions, including the answers. All Mom has to do is just read. It has lots of activities and much to pick and choose from. It is written for grades 4–8, but we have easily adjusted it to younger and older children. We are now up to the Revolutionary War, and my kids and I have been loving it!" *www.learning-adventures.org*

SCIENCE

"It's me, Darci, again. I also love *The Elements* for science. It is a really neat way to learn the elements. Each element has a picture as well as all the information about that element. The picture is supposed to represent the many facets of the element. I wish I had had this when I was taking chemistry!" *www.edgeucationpublishing.com*

"My name is Donna and I like Apologia science because it is designed for the home school! It is easy to read and done in a conversational manner, unlike many textbooks written these days. There are also some helpful printable worksheets and schedules that you can download for free to go with most of the curriculum." *www.highschoolscience.com*

"Hi, I'm Annette, and I highly recommend *Creating a Sense of Wonder* for elementary science. It really teaches us to look at our world and see the hand of God in nature. It is very user-friendly, simple to understand, and easy to teach. Best of all, it is biblically based. *www.notgrass.com*

LANGUAGE ARTS

"One homeschool resource I have loved is Sing, Spell, Read & Write. Oh, did I forget to say my name? It is Mary. Anyway, I recommend this phonics program because it is so easy and fun to teach my children to read. And spell. And write! *www.pearsonlearning.com*

"Hi, I'm Kat and I think the Reading Lesson is a great resource that introduces you and your child to reading. You have the choice of buying additional resources if you choose. I also find it great because it has beginning math available for my youngest child." *www.readinglesson.com*

"We love the reading-motivation website Book Adventure. Children in grades K–8 choose books from a book list and then take multiple-choice quizzes to earn points toward prizes. It really motivates the kids (which is a BIG plus), and the prizes are actually quite nice. The book list that the children choose from is huge—lots of great books." *www.bookadventure.com*

"*Daily Handwriting Practice: Contemporary Cursive* has been a terrific help to my son. He was never very confident about his cursive handwriting, but the practice books that I'd seen were either geared toward very young children or just so rote that practice was more of a chore than either of us wanted it to be. I was amazed at how much he liked this and how quickly his handwriting improved. The program is divided into small segments of work each day for a whole school year, which is wonderful because I think that small portions, evenly applied, are much more effective than overloading a child. Each week is centered around a fun theme, such as geography, famous inventors, animals, or sports, so the child is getting information about other things while he's practicing his writing. My son never had to be reminded to do his handwriting, and, almost immediately, he started to do all of his other work in cursive, which he had never done before." *www.evan-moor.com*

"It's Darci again and I just thought of another resource I think is wonderful. Play 'n Talk phonics curriculum has been such a wonderfully complete tool for all my needs as a homeschooling mom. As I have used it, my children have continued to grow and learn. My son now loves to read! *www.playntalk.com*

"My name is Sonya and I think *Teach Your Child to Read in 100 Easy Lessons* is an amazing resource. The lessons are short enough that a child stays focused and interested. They are simple and to the point, and each day begins with review. I think it is an excellent way to teach your child to read. *www.startreading.com*

"Hi, I'm Connie and I absolutely love A Beka literature books. They have wonderful, moral Christian stories from a wide circle of famous authors. They have them for *all* grades. They present small portions of hundreds of famous works over the years. They teach vocabulary, literary terms, and history, and ask provocative questions with thorough answers in the answer key. Every story has profound lessons; not a single word is wasted in frivolity. *www.abeka.com*

MATH

"I recommend Math U See because it takes the kids step by step and teaches them math in a fun way. They don't even realize that they are doing multiplication in the lower books because it is made so fun through songs, manipulatives, and other activities." *www.mathusee.com*

"I love Math U See because they use a hands-on approach. The blocks and videos are a great addition to this curriculum. The author, Steve Demme, does a wonderful job teaching the new concepts in the video. (I have even learned some things!) The best news is, my kids no longer hate math!"

"Hi, I'm Angie. We have used lots of different textbooks at home, but my favorite for math is the Saxon series. Math concepts are introduced very gradually, just one step a day, and lots of practice exercises are given for each new idea. The best part is the constant review Saxon provides. Our state requires standardized testing for homeschoolers, but using the Saxon series, I've never had to worry about my children's math skills meeting or exceeding the state's standards." *www.saxonhomeschool.com*

"Hello, my name is Bobbi. One resource I have loved is Singapore Math. I recommend it because it is so easy to follow that my seven-year-old son was actually learning as he did the placement exam. Beyond that, there is just enough repetition to solidify his grasp of certain concepts, and it is not so repetitious that it makes him detest math as his previous curriculum tended to do. It is also *very* economical, and the textbooks are reusable with other children. I simply have to purchase a new workbook for each child." *www.singaporemath.com*

MISCELLANEOUS RESOURCES

"My name is Tonia and my favorite resource book has been *The Well-Trained Mind* by Susan Wise Bauer. Classical education encourages children to dig deeper within themselves to relate to our ancient ancestors. Bauer has provided so many suggestions in this book that although we do not follow *everything* in this book, the resource and guidance provided is outstanding. Highly recommended! *www.welltrainedmind.com*

"Hi, I'm Shelby and one homeschooling resource I have loved is Chores and Rewards. (It has a free trial and a reasonable cost for purchase.) It has made my life so much easier. Keeping the house in order is half the battle, and it has helped keep the kids on track with chores (and can easily be used for school assignments). You can assign tasks and, if you desire, give rewards and fine the kids for their behavior. *www.choresandrewards.com*

"My name is Lynn and our family loves *God's World News* for current events. There are different age levels; it is written from a Christian perspective; maps, teacher info, and quizzes are included with this little newspaper." *www.gwnews.com*

"My name is Leslie and I'm sure many have recommended this, but one of my favorite homeschool sources is the Rainbow Resource Center. They offer an abundance of homeschool curricula and materials. Their catalog contains a detailed description of each item, written by reviewers who homeschool themselves; this, more than anything, helped me make good choices as a new homeschooling mom. Their prices are discounted and usually lower than any other sources I could purchase from." *www.rainbowresource.com*

"I too, love this catalog. My name is Linda and I have found the Rainbow Resource Center to have well-written, detailed reviews of hundreds of products that make me feel I have the product actually in my hand. That helps me make better decisions on how to spend my homeschool budget."

"My name is Nicole. The whole world is our resource, but I have found a library card and *The Unschooling Handbook* by Mary Griffith particularly essential! We are an unschooling family. A lot of people think that means we just ignore schoolwork altogether in favor of video games, but that's just not the case. For us, it means exploring whatever we find interesting and learning about life as we live it. My daughter took horseback riding lessons over the summer and found she was very interested in horses. We read about the different breeds of horses and the purposes for which they were bred, and she learned how to draw and paint horses realistically. After we found out about horses' unique nutritional needs, she discovered a recipe for horse treats on-line and baked them. She learned how to groom and train horses, and volunteered at a ranch where rescued horses are paired with abused children." *www.marygriffith.com/work1htm*

"Hi, I'm Elena and I have loved a book called *Managers of Their Homes*. There is also a website and a discussion board. The Maxwells have been a tremendous asset to our lives. I recommend it because it helps you learn and get better at managing your time when attempting to juggle all the balls of a homeschooling momma's life! It gives examples, samples, chore charts, encouragement, and great stories of experience." *www.titus2.com*

"I'm Yolanda and I just wanted to recommend a book entitled *Home Educating with Confidence* by Rick and Marilyn Boyer. I read it at the beginning of every school year, because it inspires me to believe that I can do it! The Boyers, who have homeschooled twelve children, encourage anyone that they can homeschool, too." *www.thelearningparent.com*

"Hi, I'm Tonya. Thanks for the opportunity to help. I just love mentoring new homeschool moms in this fabulous journey. One homeschool resource I have loved and recommend to all homeschooling moms is *Educating the WholeHearted Child* by Clay and Sally Clarkson. They share such refreshing detail on how to disciple our children, and isn't that what homeschooling our children is about? My favorite parts of the book are the margins full of inspiring scriptures and magnificent advice from recent and long-ago mentors of child training and discipleship." *www.wholeheart.org*

"My name is Sonya and I highly recommend the book *Polished Cornerstones*. It truly teaches a girl how to become a godly young woman, including the duties of a wife and mother. It challenges young ladies to be thoughtful and to strive for holiness." *www.doorposts.net*

"I'm Angi and my children love DLTK's Crafts for Kids! This website has lots of fun stuff for kids, including make-your-own bingo, bookmarks, and coupons, along with Bible, geography, and holiday activities." *www.dltk-kids.com*

"My name is Joyce and our favorite website is San Diego Homeschooling. It offers information in the San Diego area, including reviews on homeschooling curriculum, field trips, and many more resources for families." *www.homeschoolreview.com*

"I'm Christy and our family cannot school without large world and U.S. maps! We have learned so much simply by looking up where news is happening and where books take place, tracking hurricanes, etc. It is invaluable!"

"My name is Stephanie and we often visit the Sites for Teachers website. We have found hundreds of free printables, curriculum, and homeschooling links. We went a year without curriculum because of financial difficulties. This website kept us alive! *www.sitesforteachers.com*

These are real people offering their personal opinions when asked which resource they would most recommend to someone considering homeschooling. If you have a favorite resource you want to recommend, please visit me at www.lisawhelchel.com and tell me about it. Or just click on the homeschool section and learn what others are recommending!

GET THE REAL "FACTS OF LIFE"

America grew up learning *The Facts of Life* on this popular television sitcom of the 1980s. As Blair Warner, rich, pampered boarding school student, Lisa Whelchel matured from a snobby prep schooler to a responsible adult. Now the actress recounts the real facts of life she's learned as a child of God making the journey—from a shy girl out of a small town in Texas, to the glamorous life of fame and fortune in Hollywood, to suburban life as a pastor's wife and homeschooling mother of three. Readers will relish this inside glimpse into the life of a child star who looks to her Heavenly Father. Touching autobiographical stories reveal the developing trust in God that has enabled Lisa to grow in grace through seasons of pressure, pain, and prosperity.

ISBN 1-57673-858-2